BAU

ZAGATSURVEY®

SPRING 2003

NEW YORK CITY THEATER GUIDE

Editor: Troy Segal

Published and distributed by
ZAGAT SURVEY, LLC
4 Columbus Circle
New York, New York 10019
Tel: 212 977 6000
E-mail: theaterbook@zagat.com
Web site: www.zagat.com

Acknowledgments

We thank the following, without whose help this guide would not have been possible: Jed Bernstein, John Breglio, Peter Filichia, Henry Guettel, Gail Horwood, Marc Miller, Richard Norton, Steve Shukow, Peter J. Solomon, Ron Spivak and Dick Tofel.

We also thank our staff, especially Reni Chin, Larry Cohn, Liz Daleske, Steve DeLorenzo, Griff Foxley, Jeff Freier, Curt Gathje, Tricia Heinz, Natalie Lebert, Mike Liao, Dave Makulec, Shari Matsuo, Lorraine Mead, Laura Mitchell, Emily Parsons, Rob Seixas, Daniel Simmons, Erinn Stivala and Kyle Zolner, for their work on this project.

Contents

About This Survey

With this new thrice-yearly guide, and the cooperation of *The Wall Street Journal,* we are fulfilling a long-cherished dream of covering a quintessential New York City activity – theatergoing. Based on our 24 years of reporting on the shared experiences of NYC diners, travelers, nightlife aficionados and, of late, shoppers, we believe the theater is an especially appropriate area for our approach of engaging the customer – in this case the audience – in an evaluation process, by analyzing the shows they see.

One thing is clear – by surveying thousands of members of the public, Zagat Survey offers a take on the theater that's different from the opinions of a single professional critic. As our *Survey* audience's ratings and comments indicate, paying customers have an overwhelmingly positive perception. Quite simply, the lay public enjoys the theater more than the professional reviewers seem to, perhaps because for most, play-going is a pleasure rather than a job. Not that critics don't love the theater. But their task is, by nature as well as name, critical. And having to see virtually everything that's staged often makes their responses seem jaded, and their judgments, expressed as "an authority", harsher than those of the audience, who simply aim to be entertained. Most shows seem to do that. When we asked our voters the ultimate question, "would you recommend this show?", 75% of them said "yes" to over three-quarters of the productions – and, amazingly, 90% recommended at least one out of three shows. Reflecting the high degree of the NYC theater's professionalism, virtually no show is recommended by less than half its audience.

By recording such enthusiastic sentiment here, we aim to put some bite into the buzz, providing an alternative to the critics' views. Too often nowadays, if a production doesn't please the *New York Times* critic, his negative review can kill that show. This is not meant as an attack on the *Times* or its critics, but simply reflects the influence of that great paper in this field. Through this guide and our weekly column in the *WSJ,* we plan to codify and quickly communicate the audience word-of-mouth, to give deserving new shows a better chance of survival. If we can do this, we believe the theater as a whole will be healthier.

Not that our surveyors don't have some complaints about theatergoing. Close to half of them (44%) are put off by the high prices of Broadway today – which explains why 70%

say they always or often pursue discounts (the TKTS ticket booths in Times Square and the South Street Seaport are especially popular options, patronized by 45% of surveyors). The second biggest beef, held by 20% of surveyors, is cramped seating. If theater owners want to fill those seats, perhaps they should pay a little more attention to their size, à la the taxi industry's recently enlarged back seats.

As mentioned above, this Spring edition of our *Theater Survey* is the first in a thrice-yearly series (the next is scheduled for August). It covers 57 current productions both on and Off-Broadway. Besides rating and reviewing each show, we have listed theater addresses, phone numbers, casts and credits, and – because 55% of you say you purchase tickets over the Internet – Web sites. Because an overwhelming 90% of our respondents say they usually dine out when going to a show, we've included a section of restaurants culled from our *NYC Restaurants Survey* and another of nightlife venues from our *NYC Nightlife Survey*. These places are situated in the Theater District on the West Side or in other neighborhoods convenient to clusters of Off-Broadway houses.

The shows covered herein were rated separately on the quality of their Acting, Story and Production by 8,625 surveyors, who see an average 15.4 shows a year. Of these participants, 59% are women. The breakdown by age is: 20% in their 20s; 21%, 30s; 20%, 40s; 25%, 50s; and 14%, 60s and above. As with all our guides, we've synopsized our surveyors' opinions, with their comments shown in quotation marks. We sincerely thank each of our participants; this book is really "theirs."

To aid your theatergoing, we have also prepared a number of maps and lists, not only of the top shows (beginning on page 15), but also of the leading restaurants (page 61), nightlife (page 99), hotels (page 116) and even parking facilities – which should hearten the 12% of our surveyors who find parking a major irritant. Finally, we have included theater seating charts (page 35) and handy indexes, so that you can find the right show as well as the right seat.

Since this *Survey* is a first-time effort, we would appreciate your comments, and even criticisms, so that we can improve future editions. Contact us at theaterbook@zagat.com. To vote and receive a free copy of our next *Theater Survey*, just go to zagat.com and click on the "theater" link. We look forward to hearing from you.

New York, NY
May 12, 2003

Nina and Tim Zagat

Showbuzz

At long last, spring has arrived, and Broadway and Off-Broadway are abloom with shows to captivate theater-goers: 12 new productions have hit the boards in April alone. This, the premiere of our *Theater Survey,* gives surveyors' recommendations, ratings and reviews for shows that are either open or previewing as of press time. What follows here is an overview of the NYC theater scene both currently and over the coming few months.

Musicals Rule: Given the variety of winter storms – political, economic and natural – it's not surprising that escapist entertainment predominates: Nearly half the productions playing right now are musicals or musical revues. And with many of the season's surprise new hits – *Avenue Q, The Play What I Wrote* and *Zanna, Don't!* – the message is mainly one of risqué fun or, in the case of the kids' show *A Year With Frog and Toad,* just plain fun. Even more musical notes will be struck soon: The 1982 show *Big River* will rise again this summer, in a production mounted by the Deaf West Theatre that uses both hearing and hearing-impaired actors to sing and sign the adventures of Huckleberry Finn and Jim on that floating raft. The campy classic *Little Shop of Horrors,* about a carnivorous plant from another planet, will also be open for business in July; the cast includes Lee Wilkof, who starred in the original 1982 production.

Serious Sells: It isn't all frothy fare, however. Some provocative works dealing with such issues as capital punishment (*The Exonerated*) or finding humor in a handicapped child (*A Day in the Death of Joe Egg*) are thriving too. Often, to sell such shows, you gotta get a gimmick, as they sing in the new revival of *Gypsy.* It can be telling three variants on the same story, as does *Life (x) 3,* or presenting a series of soliloquies, in alternating programs, like *Talking Heads* – to name two recent premieres so successful that they've already extended their original limited runs.

Stargazing: Of course, the most time-honored gimmick of all is to have famous names on the marquee. Almost half of Zagat surveyors – 48% – say they're more likely to see a show that features celebrities. And when polled specifically about their favorite performers, they named, in order of popularity (current show in parentheses): **Men:** Nathan Lane, Brian Stokes Mitchell (*Man of La Mancha*), Michael Crawford, Matthew Broderick, Adam Pascal (*Aida*), Mandy Patinkin, Harvey Fierstein (*Hairspray*), Alan Cumming, Colm Wilkinson and Terence Mann. **Women:** Bernadette Peters (*Gypsy*), Julie Andrews, Bebe Neuwirth (the upcoming *Writer's Block*), Barbra Streisand, Patti Lupone, Heather Headley, Lea Salonga, Betty Buckley, Audra McDonald and

Linda Eder. If the star's the thing, there'll soon be plenty of other must-sees on surveyors' lists. Singer Toni Braxton is assuming the title role in *Aida* for four months in June. Melanie Griffith will make her Broadway bow in *Chicago,* as the murderous flapper Roxie Hart, playing opposite (i.e. across 49th Street) husband Antonio Banderas, star of the hit revival of *Nine.* Other visitors from the Hollywood hills head the cast of *Eugene O'Neill's Long Day's Journey into Night,* with Vanessa Redgrave and Brian Dennehy portraying the parents of the tortured Tyrone family, and Robert Sean Leonard and Philip Seymour Hoffman their sons.

The Playwright's the Thing: With other newcomers, the best-known name is not on the stage, but behind it. Film director and writer Woody Allen's first success was actually a play (*Play It Again, Sam*), and now he returns to the boards – and makes his directorial debut – with two one-acts, presented under the title *Writer's Block.* Cartoonist Jules Feiffer, who also has periodically dipped his pen into playwrighting, is offering *A Bad Friend,* scheduled for spring: It concerns a Brooklyn family that has Communist leanings in 1953 – not a good year to be a Red. The Manhattan Theatre Club is presenting the world premiere of *Last Dance,* by Marsha Norman, best-known for her Pulitzer Prize-winning *'Night, Mother,* this somewhat cheerier work depicts a poet beseiged by sycophants in her Riviera villa.

Provocative Productions: The Manhattan Theatre Club is also producing the American premiere of *Humble Boy,* a recent London hit that reworks *Hamlet,* turning the troubled prince into an astrophysicist coming home for the funeral of his father, a noted beekeeper. For those who prefer their Shakespeare straight, there's *Henry V,* this summer's Shakespeare-in-the-Park offering; Liev Schreiber, who recently starred in the Public Theater's *Othello,* plays the soldier-king. The life of another Renaissance man is imaginatively depicted in *The Notebooks of Leonardo da Vinci;* adaptor and director Mary Zimmerman, the force behind last year's hit *Metamorphoses,* uses an innovative blend of song, dance and gymnastics to dramatize the artist/inventor's ideas and theories. Also on hand is a revival of South African playwright Athol Fugard's 1982 *"Master Harold" . . . and the Boys,* about a teenager and his family's two black servants, with original cast members Danny Glover and Lonny Price. But what a difference two decades makes: Glover now plays the older employee, and Price, who created the title role, now directs.

Going Solo: Several one-man acts are in the works. First up is Bill Maher (ex TV's *Politically Incorrect*), who shares his often-controversial commentary on domestic and foreign affairs in *Victory Begins at Home.* The true story of an East German transvestite who survived both the Nazi and the

Communist regimes is the subject of *I Am My Own Wife,* a new piece penned by Douglas Wright, who wrote the play and movie *Quills,* and directed by Moisés Kaufman (*The Laramie Project*).

Final Bows: The vernal rejuvenation is especially welcome, because this winter has been especially tough for theater. Several newcomers, including *Adult Entertainment, Showtune* and *Vincent in Brixton,* all posted earlier-than-expected closing notices, and *Urban Cowboy* is struggling in the saddle. Broadway is also bidding good-bye to two veterans: the 16-year-old *Tony N' Tina's Wedding* (though the producers plan to re-open when they renovate their venue) and *Les Misérables,* at 6,680 performances the second-longest-running production in the Great White Way's history. However, given the numbers of folks who would be miserable without it – the musical still scores a recommendation rate of 93% from the 3,857 Zagat surveyors who saw it – maybe it's not too early to start planning the revival.

Spontaneous Show-Going: It's no secret that advance sales are down for many shows: According to a League of American Theatres and Producers' demographic study, 38% of audiences buy their tickets less than one week in advance (and another 25% buy within a month of attendance). Maybe such news makes producers nervous, but for theatergoers, it means that seeing a show can be more of an impulse buy, with seats often available even for established hits. Furthermore, it's never been easier to get tickets at a discount. There are the TKTS booths of course, but also several Web sites, such as broadwaybox.com, hitshowclub.com, nytheatre.com, playbill.com and theatermania.com, which regularly feature deals on both Broadway and Off-Broadway offerings. For a modest fee, eligible patrons can also join non-profit organizations such as the Theatre Development Fund (tdf.org) and the Drama League (dramaleague.org), which regularly offer members reduced – sometimes even free – tickets.

On With the Show: Available seats, discount deals, celebrity stars and a host of new offerings that range from Henry V to Huckleberry Finn – there's no reason not to get out and see a show. Will any of the above-mentioned newcomers develop 'legs,' as they say in the biz? Only time – and the next edition of our *Theater Survey* – will tell.

New York, NY   Troy Segal
May 12, 2003

Preview

The following are shows whose curtains were going up as this guide was coming out. Dates indicating first preview (P) and opening night (O) precede each show's name.

5/2 (O) **Streakin'**, Babalu, 323 W. 44th St., 212-279-4200 (TS) *By Jamie Rocco & Albert Evans; director & choreographer, Jamie Rocco.*

5/5 (O) **Bill Maher's Victory Begins At Home**, Virginia, 245 W. 52nd St., 212-239-6200 (TC) *Written & performed by Bill Maher.*

5/6 (O) **Long Day's Journey Into Night**, Plymouth, 236 W. 45th St., 212-239-6200 (TC) *With Brian Dennehy, Vanessa Redgrave, Philip Seymour Hoffman & Robert Sean Leonard; by Eugene O'Neill.*

5/8 (O) **Cavedweller**, NY Theatre Workshop, 79 E. 4th St., 212-239-6200 (TC) *By Kate Moira Ryan; director, Michael Greif.*

5/15 (O) **Writer's Block**, Atlantic Theater Co., 336 W. 20th St., 212-239-6200 (TC) *With Paul Reiser & Bebe Neuwirth; written & directed by Woody Allen.*

5/18 (O) **Humble Boy**, City Center, 131 W. 55th St., 212-581-1212 (TS) *By Charlotte Jones; director, John Caird.*

5/2 (P); 5/22 (O) **I Am My Own Wife**, Playwrights Horizons, 416 W. 42nd St., 212-279-4200 (TS) *By Doug Wright; director, Moisés Kaufman.*

5/6 (P); 6/1 (O) **"Master Harold" . . . and the Boys**, Royale, 242 W. 45th St., 212-239-6200 (TC) *With Danny Glover; by Athol Fugard; director, Lonny Price.*

5/6 (P); 6/3 (O) **Last Dance**, City Center, 131 W. 55th St., 212-581-1212 (TS) *By Marsha Norman; director, Lynne Meadow.*

5/15 (P); 6/9 (O) **A Bad Friend**, Mitzi E. Newhouse, 150 W. 65th St., 212-239-6200 (TC) *By Jules Feiffer; director, Jerry Zaks.*

5/21 (P); 6/11 (O) **Intrigue with Faye**, Acorn, 410 W. 42nd St., 212-279-4200 (TS) *With Benjamin Bratt & Julianna Marguilies; by Kate Robin.*

6/3 (P); 6/19 (O) **Notebooks of Leonardo Da Vinci**, Second Stage, 307 W. 43rd St., 212-246-4422 (BO) *Adapted & directed by Mary Zimmerman.*

6/24 (P); 7/15 (O) **Henry V**, Delacorte, Central Park, 212-539-8750 (info) *With Liev Schreiber; by William Shakespeare.*

TBA **Big River**, American Airlines, 227 W. 42nd St., 212-719-1300 (info) *Book, William Hauptman; music & lyrics, Roger Miller.*

7/16 (P); 8/14 (O) **Little Shop of Horrors**, Virginia, 245 W. 52nd St., TBA *Book & lyrics, Howard Ashman; music, Alan Menken.*

The Theater District

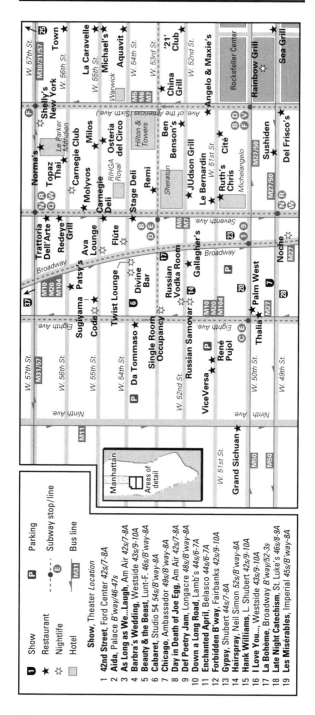

Show, Theater *Location*

1. **42nd Street**, Ford Center *42s/7-8A*
2. **Aida**, Palace *B'way/46-47s*
3. **As Long as We...Laugh**, Am Air *42s/7-8A*
4. **Barbra's Wedding**, Westside *43s/9-10A*
5. **Beauty & the Beast**, Lunt-F. *46s/B'way-8A*
6. **Cabaret**, Studio 54 *54s/B'way-8A*
7. **Chicago**, Ambassador *49s/B'way-8A*
8. **Day in Death of Joe Egg**, Am Air *42s/7-8A*
9. **Def Poetry Jam**, Longacre *48s/B'way-8A*
10. **Down a Long Road**, Lamb's *44s/6-7A*
11. **Enchanted April**, Belasco *44s/6-7A*
12. **Forbidden B'way**, Fairbanks *42s/9-10A*
13. **Gypsy**, Shubert *44s/7-8A*
14. **Hairspray**, Neil Simon *52s/B'way-8A*
15. **Hank Williams**, L. Shubert *42s/9-10A*
16. **I Love You...**, Westside *43s/9-10A*
17. **La Bohème**, Broadway *B'way/52-3s*
18. **Late Night Catechism**, St. Luke's *46s/8-9A*
19. **Les Misérables**, Imperial *45s/B'way-8A*

The Theater District

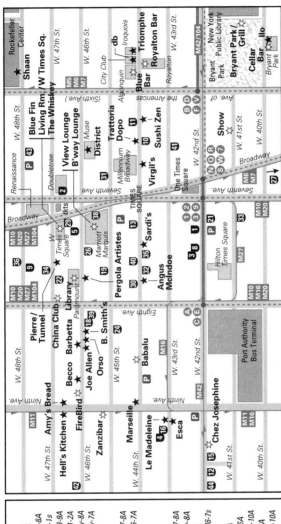

Union Square and The Village

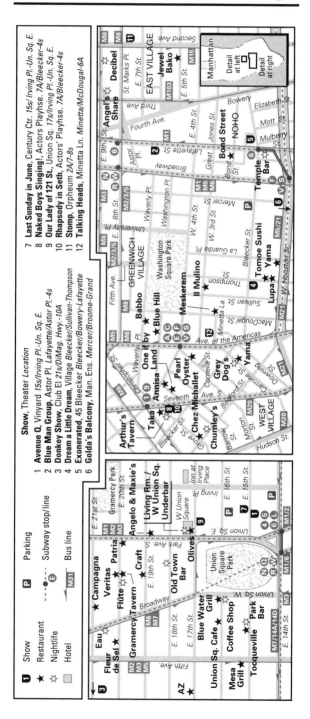

Show, Theater Location

1 **Avenue Q**, Vinyard 15s/Irving Pl.-Un. Sq. E.
2 **Blue Man Group**, Astor Pl. Lafayette/Astor Pl.-4s
3 **Donkey Show**, Club El 21s/DiMag. Hwy.-10A
4 **Dream a Little Dream**, Village Bleecker/Sullivan-Thompson
5 **Exonerated**, 45 Bleecker Bleecker/Bowery-Lafayette
6 **Golda's Balcony**, Man. Ens. Mercer/Broome-Grand
7 **Last Sunday in June**, Century Ctr. 15s/Irving Pl.-Un. Sq. E.
8 **Naked Boys Singing!**, Actors Playhse. 7A/Bleecker-4s
9 **Our Lady of 121 St.**, Union Sq. 17s/Irving Pl.-Un. Sq. E.
10 **Rhapsody in Seth**, Actors' Playhse. 7A/Bleecker-4s
11 **Stomp**, Orpheum 2A/7-8s
12 **Talking Heads**, Minetta Ln. Minetta/McDougal-6A

T Show
★ Restaurant
☆ Nightlife
▢ Hotel

P Parking
---•E--- Subway stop/line
M31 Bus line

Current Shows

Key to Ratings/Symbols

% Recommending, Show, Theater & Address,
Reservation No., Web Site, Cast & Credits

Zagat Ratings

Unusual Show Times

A	S	P

100% Tim & Nina's Show 🄢🄜   ▽ 23 | 9 | 13

Survey Center, 4001 Broadway (48th St.), 212-977-6000 (TC);
www.zagat.com
*With Tim & Nina Zagat; book, music & lyrics by Ted
Zagat; director, John Zagat.*

◪ Now in its 24th year, this "long-running" "family show"
thrives, despite an "impossible story" of "two entrepreneurs
running wild" and "poor" production values ("the whole
set consists of blow-ups of old Zagat Guide covers"); the
secret to its success lies in the "jovial leads" Tim and Nina,
who are so "eager to please" they "pay you to stay" until
their curtain calls.

Review, with surveyors' comments in quotes

Before reviews a symbol indicates whether responses were
uniform ■ or mixed ◪.

Unusual Show Times: 🄢 plays Sunday night
🄜 plays Monday night

Reservation Numbers: TM = TicketMaster
TC = Telecharge
TS = other ticket service
BO = box office

Ratings: Acting, Story and Production Values are rated on
a scale of **0** to **30**.

A	Acting	S	Story	P	Production

23 | 9 | 13

0–9	poor to fair	**20–25**	very good to excellent
10–15	fair to good	**26–30**	extraordinary to perfection
16–19	good to very good	▽	low response/less reliable

Shows listed without ratings were in preview at the time
this guide went to press. In such cases, the opening date
appears in parentheses after the show's name.

Highly Recommended*

REC	B'WAY MUSICAL	A	S	P
95%	Hairspray, *Neil Simon* (TM)	27	24	28
	The Producers, *St. James* (TC)	26	26	27
94%	Cabaret, *Studio 54* (TC)	24	25	25
	The Lion King, *New Amsterdam* (TM)	23	22	29
93%	Les Misérables, *Imperial* (TC)	25	26	27
92%	42nd Street, *Ford Center* (TM)	22	19	26
	Chicago, *Ambassador* (TC)	24	23	25
91%	Beauty & the Beast, *Lunt-Fontanne* (TM)	21	22	25
88%	Phantom of the Opera, *Majestic* (TC)	23	23	26
	Nine, *Eugene O'Neill* (TC)	26	20	24
	La Bohème, *Broadway* (TC)	23	24	26
87%	Mamma Mia!, *Cadillac Winter Garden* (TC)	22	17	24
	Thoroughly Modern Millie, *Marquis* (TM)	24	20	25
86%	Man of La Mancha, *Martin Beck* (TC)	24	23	23
85%	Aida, *Palace* (TM)	23	21	25
81%	Urinetown: The Musical, *Henry Miller's* (TC)	24	21	22
80%	Rent, *Nederlander* (TM)	22	22	22
75%	Movin' Out, *Richard Rogers* (TM)	20	15	23

REC	OFF B'WAY MUSICAL/REVUE	A	S	P
96%	Hank Williams: Lost Highway, *Little Shubert* (TC)	26	24	25
94%	Dream A Little Dream, *Village* (TM)	25	25	25
91%	Menopause The Musical, *Playhouse 91* (BO)	22	22	21
90%	Forbidden Broadway, *Fairbanks* (TC)	22	19	19
90%	Blue Man Group: Tubes, *Astor Place* (BO)	22	15	25
89%	Avenue Q, *Vineyard* (TC)	25	23	25
87%	Zanna, Don't!, *John Houseman* (TC)	23	20	22
85%	Stomp, *Orpheum* (BO)	18	13	23
84%	I Love You, You're Perfect, *Westside* (TC)	20	20	18
80%	Naked Boys Singing!, *Actors' Playhouse* (TC)	17	13	17
70%	Donkey Show, *Club El Flamingo* (TM)	14	14	18

REC	COMEDY	A	S	P
93%	Say Goodnight Gracie, *Helen Hayes* (TC)	27	23	21
86%	Late Night Catechism, *St. Luke's* (TC)	22	19	17
77%	Tony N' Tina's Wedding, *St. Luke's* (BO)	17	17	18
	The Play What I Wrote, *Lyceum* (TC)	23	15	20
69%	Life (x) 3, *Circle in the Square* (TC)	25	16	21

REC	DRAMA	A	S	P
94%	The Exonerated, *45 Bleecker* (TM)	25	27	21
91%	Take Me Out, *Walter Kerr* (TC)	26	23	25
89%	Tea at Five, *Promenade* (TC)	27	18	21
	Golda's Balcony, *Manhattan Ensemble* (TC)	27	24	24
87%	Day in the Death of Joe Egg, *American Air.* (TS)	27	23	22
82%	Russell Simmons' Def Poetry Jam, *Longacre* (TC)	23	18	20
81%	Our Lady of 121st Street, *Union Square* (TM)	25	18	20

* By at least 2/3 of the audience
TM (TicketMaster) = 212-307-4100; TC (Telecharge) = 212-239-6200;
TS (other ticket service) = see Directory of Current Shows;
BO = call box office

Top Ratings

By Genre

Adaptation
95% Hairspray
    Producers
94% Lion King
    Les Misérables
92% 42nd Street

Campy
95% Hairspray
91% Menopause
87% Mamma Mia
    Zanna, Don't
78% Naked Boys

Dancing Feet
95% Producers
94% Cabaret
92% 42nd Street
    Chicago
75% Movin' Out

Deeply Moving
94% Exonerated
    Cabaret
92% Talking Heads
87% Joe Egg
82% Women of Lockerbie

Evergreen
95% Producers
94% Cabaret
    Lion King
93% Les Misérables
92% 42nd Street

Family Fun
95% Hairspray
94% Lion King
91% Beauty & Beast
90% Blue Man Group
87% Thoroughly MM

Fast-Starters▽
94% Year with Frog . . .
92% Talking Heads
91% Rhapsody in Seth
82% Women of Lockerbie
75% Last Sunday in June

Limited Runs
89% Golda's Balcony
88% Nine
87% Joe Egg
82% Women of Lockerbie
70% Life (x) 3

Lots of Laughs
93% Say G'dnight Gracie
86% Late Night Catechism
77% Tony N' Tina's Wedding
75% Last Sunday in June
    Play What I Wrote

Love Stories
93% Les Misérables
    Say G'dnight Gracie
88% Phantom of Opera
    Nine
    La Bohème

Nostalgic Appeal
96% Hank Williams
94% Dream a Little Dream
93% Say G'dnight Gracie
92% 42nd Street
88% Tea at Five

Revivals
94% Cabaret
92% 42nd Street
    Chicago
88% Nine
87% Joe Egg

Songfests
96% Hank Williams
88% La Bohème
87% Mamma Mia
86% Man of La Mancha
85% Aida

Star Turns
95% Hairspray
94% Cabaret
93% Say G'dnight Gracie
92% Talking Heads
89% Tea at Five

Top Ratings

By Acting

27 Golda's Balcony (D)
    Tea at Five (D)
    Hairspray (M)
    Say G'dnight Gracie (C)
    Joe Egg (D)
26 Producers (M)
    Take Me Out (D)
    Nine (M)
    Hank Williams (M)
25 Exonerated (D)

    Avenue Q (M)
    Life (x) 3 (C)
    Les Mis (M)
    Dream A Little Dream (R)
24 Chicago (M)
    Cabaret (M)
    Man of La Mancha (M)
    Urinetown (M)
    Thoroughly MM (M)
23 La Bohème (M)

By Story

27 Exonerated (D)
26 Les Mis (M)
    Producers (M)
25 Dream a Little Dream (R)
    Cabaret (M)
24 Golda's Balcony (D)
    Hairspray (M)
    La Bohème (M)
    Hank Williams (M)
23 Chicago (M)

    Take Me Out (D)
    Phantom of Opera (M)
    Man of La Mancha (M)
    Joe Egg (D)
    Say G'dnight Gracie (C)
    Avenue Q (M)
22 Lion King (M)
    Beauty & Beast (M)
    Menopause (M)
    Rent (M)

By Production Values

29 Lion King (M)
28 Hairspray (M)
27 Producers (M)
    Les Misérables (M)
26 42nd Street (M)
    La Bohème (M)
    Phantom of Opera (M)
25 Cabaret (M)
    Dream a Little Dream (R)
    Beauty & Beast (M)

    Chicago (M)
    Hank Williams (M)
    Aida (M)
    Blue Man Group (P)
    Avenue Q (M)
    Thoroughly MM (M)
    Take Me Out (D)
24 Golda's Balcony (D)
    Nine (M)
    Mamma Mia (M)

C=Comedy, D=Drama, M=Musical, P=Performance, R=Revue

85% **Aida**   23   21   25

Palace, 1564 Broadway (bet. 46th & 47th Sts.), 212-307-4100 (TM); disney.go.com

With Saycon Senybloh, Felicia Finley & Adam Pascal; book, Linda Woolverton & David Henry Hwang; music, Elton John; lyrics, Tim Rice; director, Robert Falls.

☑ A "retelling" of the "great Verdi opera's" "tear-jerker" tale of "star-crossed lovers", this "technologically brilliant" "spectacular" ("fabulous costumes", "imaginative sets", "extraordinary lighting") features "three excellent leads", as well as a "Disneyfied" "surprise ending" that "hits a happy note"; some find Sir Elton's "melodic pop-rock score" a bit "repetitive" and fault a few "pointless production numbers", but for most this "guilty pleasure" is "like candy" – full of "empty calories but delicious" nonetheless.

61% **As Long as We Both**   ∇ 18   14   14
Shall Laugh S M

American Airlines, 227 W. 42nd St. (bet. 7th & 8th Aves.), 212-719-1300 (TS); www.roundabouttheatre.org

Conceived and performed by Yakov Smirnoff.

☑ "It isn't a joke" – the Russian "stand-up comic" "Yakov Smirnoff really is doing a Broadway show" (two nights a week, anyway); but while this one-man effort, which describes his immigration to the U.S., his marriage and the relations between men and women, strikes supporters as "good for a light, entertaining evening", obviously at least one-third isn't laughing, finding the routines "based on the quirks of American culture" "a little stale."

89% **Avenue Q** S   25   23   25

Vineyard, 108 E. 15th St. (bet. Irving Pl. & Union Sq. E.), 212-239-6200 (TC); www.vineyardtheatre.org

With an ensemble cast; book, Jeff Whitty; music & lyrics, Robert Lopez & Jeff Marx; director, Jason Moore.

■ "Humor, pathos, puppets having sex" – "this show has something for everyone (except the kids)" say patrons about this "part paen to puppetry, part urban-life statement" and part "knowing satire of [children's] shows' ("like *The Muppets* meets *South Park*"); as it "weaves the story" of several stuffed friends "and their human counterparts" coping in the big city, the "imaginative" production boasts plenty of "catchy songs" and "hysterically funny" situations "with a sweet heart underneath"; N.B. it's scheduled to move to the Golden Theatre (252 W. 45th Street) in July.

39% **Barbra's Wedding** S   18   10   14

Westside, 407 W. 43rd St. (bet. 9th & 10th Aves.), 212-239-6200 (TC); www.barbraswedding.com

With John Pankow & Julie White; by Daniel Stern; director, David Warren.

☑ "Barbra Streisand is getting married, and the events are driving her [uninvited] neighbor crazy" in this "two-character" comedy that marks the inauspicious playwriting debut of actor Daniel Stern; while fans find actors John Pankow (*Mad About You*) and Julie White (*Six Feet Under*) "entertaining", most show-goers say the story is "too drawn out" and "would've worked better as a one-hour TV show."

91% Beauty and the Beast ⑤   21 22 25
Lunt-Fontanne, 205 W. 46th St. (bet. B'way & 8th Ave.), 212-307-4100 (TM); disney.go.com
With Steve Blanchard & Megan McGinnis; book, Linda Woolverton; music, Alan Menken; lyrics, Howard Ashman & Tim Rice; director, Robert Jess Roth.
■ The "first show" to work "Disney magic" on the Great White Way, this "beautifully realized" "adaptation" is "faithful" to the fairy-tale film, "bringing the story to life" via "catchy music" (including some "great songs not in the movie"), "colorful costumes" and "dazzling special effects" ("just how do they transform beast into prince right before your eyes?"); though a few feel it "doesn't live up to" the "beloved cartoon", the "mesmerized" majority maintains this "tale as old as time" "will go on forever."

90% Blue Man Group: Tubes ⑤   22 15 25
Astor Place, 434 Lafayette St. (bet. Astor Pl. & E. 4th St.), 212-254-4370 (BO); www.blueman.com
With alternating casts; composed, written & directed, Matt Goldman, Phil Stanton & Chris Wink; co-director, Marlene Swartz.
■ For an "original" way to beat the blues, theatergoers tout this 12-year-old "alternative-theater mainstay", "a combination of rock concert and performance art"; "there's no story", just an "outrageous collection of skits" featuring "amazing audio-visuals" and three mute, indigo-hued men playing makeshift instruments, spurting food and splattering paint ("wear your raincoat if you're in the first rows"); it's behavior that "you'd ban at home, but is fun to watch" onstage – "especially with children" or out-of-town guests.

94% Cabaret Ⓜ   24 25 25
Studio 54, 254 W. 54th St. (bet. B'way & 8th Ave.), 212-239-6200 (TC); www.cabaret-54.com
With Neil Patrick Harris, Deborah Gibson, Tom Bosley & Mariette Hartley; book, Joe Masteroff; music, John Kander; lyrics, Fred Ebb; director, Sam Mendes; choreographer, Rob Marshall.
⊠ "Searing" yet "endearing", this "fast-paced picture of cultural decay" in 1930s Berlin is "still going strong after five years", thanks to Kander and Ebb's "splendid" score and a "rotating cast of stars"; a revival that's "raunchier than the original", it comes with "sexy" dancing, a "more explicit" book, "decadently" disheveled costumes and other "in-your-face tactics" – presented in the converted Studio 54 "nightclub setting" where you sit at tables and drink "overpriced champagne" as at a real cabaret; "don't expect a happy ending, but do expect one hot performance."

92% Chicago 🅂🅜   24 | 23 | 25
Ambassador, 219 W. 49th St. (bet. B'way & 8th Ave.),
212-239-6200 (TC); www.chicagothemusical.com
With Belle Calaway, Brenda Braxton & Clarke Peters; book,
Fred Ebb & Bob Fosse; music, John Kander; lyrics, Fred Ebb;
director, Walter Bobbie; choreographer, Ann Reinking.
■ The Academy Award-winning "film overshadows it now",
but devotees declare "nothing compares to seeing in the
flesh the razzle-dazzle" of this "sexy stunner", a "stripped-
down version of the classic 1975 show"; the "bare-bones
production features amazing dancing" ("Ann Reinking's
tribute to Bob Fosse") to tell "a cynical story" about Jazz
Age murderesses-turned-media-darlings; as they slither
through Kander and Ebb's "jazzy", "seething" numbers,
the "talented, fit cast" "will inspire you to go to the gym"
after you emerge from the theater.

87% Day in the Death of Joe Egg, A   27 | 23 | 22
American Airlines, 227 W. 42nd St. (bet. 7th & 8th Aves.),
212-719-1300 (TS); www.roundabouttheatre.org
With Eddie Izzard & Victoria Hamilton; by Peter Nichols;
director, Laurence Boswell.
■ You wouldn't think the story of "a couple dealing with a
severely disabled child" could be the stuff of "stand-up
humor", but this "mesmerizing" 1968 British "jet-black
comedy" manages to be just that – and "deeply moving" as
well; Peter Nichols' dialogue ranges from "heartbreaking
to hilarious", especially as interpreted by leads Eddie
Izzard and Victoria Hamilton, re-creating their "must-see
performances" from the recent London revival.

70% Donkey Show, The   14 | 14 | 18
Club El Flamingo, 547 W. 21st St. (bet Joe DiMaggio Hwy. &
10th Ave.), 212-307-4100 (TM); www.thedonkeyshow.com
With an ensemble cast; created & directed by Diane
Paulus & Randy Weiner.
◪ "The big dance clubs of the '70s" live again in this flashy,
"campy" "disco retelling of *A Midsummer Night's Dream*"
that encourages audiences to sing along to the pre-recorded
period hits; most surveyors say it's "fun for a bachelorette
party or birthday" as long as you "bring your dancing
shoes", but a disgruntled minority mutters "the donkeys
in this show are the audience"; N.B. Friday–Saturday only.

— Down a Long Road (Open 5/14)   – | – | –
Lamb's, 130 W. 44th St. (bet. 6th & 7th Aves.), 212-239-6200 (TC);
www.downalongroad.com
Written & performed by David Marquis; director, Doug Jackson.
Educator, performer and peace activist David Marquis –
best-known for his solo show *I Am a Teacher* – uses song,
story and a few dance steps to "draw you into his journeys"
around the Third World, with detours down memory lane to
his Lubbock, Texas, childhood; his "thought-provoking"

autobiographical wanderings are accompanied by a three-piece band, whose "good music" magically evokes every place from Pakistan to the Philippines.

94% Dream a Little Dream Ⓜ   25 | 25 | 25
Village Theater, 158 Bleecker St. (bet. Sullivan & Thompson Sts.), 212-307-4100 (TM); www.mamasandpapasmusical.com
With Denny Doherty; by Paul Ledoux; music & lyrics, The Mamas & The Papas; director, Randal Myler.
■ No, you're not California Dreamin' – that *is* Denny Doherty, "an original papa" from The Mamas and the Papas; backed by a "brilliant band and singers" and some spiffy slides, he's offering a "time-traveling therapy session" that traces the beloved group's "decadent lifestyle"; it's a "flashback-inducing" trip that "makes you want to dust off the old LPs."

— Enchanted April (Open 4/29)   – | – | –
Belasco, 111 W. 44th St. (bet. 6th & 7th Aves.), 212-239-6200 (TC)
With Molly Ringwald, Elizabeth Ashley, Jayne Atkinson & Dagmara Dominczyk; by Matthew Barber; director, Michael Wilson.
A starry female cast heads this "charming", "well-acted" new period piece, based – like the lushly romantic 1992 movie of the same name – on a 1922 novel, about a quartet of drooping English roses who blossom when they rent a Tuscan villa one spring; veteran actors Michael Cumpsty (*42nd Street*), Michael Hayden (*Carousel*) and Daniel Gerroll (*Shanghai Moon*) are among the men in their lives, who also fall under the spell of the Italian sun; N.B. previewing at press time, it's set to open at the end of – naturally – April.

94% Exonerated, The Ⓢ   25 | 27 | 21
45 Bleecker, 45 Bleecker St. (bet. Bowery & Lafayette St.), 212-307-4100 (TM); www.45bleecker.com
With a rotating celebrity cast; by Jessica Blank & Erik Jensen; director, Bob Balaban.
■ "A must-see for believers and non-believers in capital punishment" alike, this "bare-bones" yet "bone-chilling" drama consists of "10 actors (three of whom are rotating celebrities) sitting and reading from scripts that tell, in their own words, of people put on death row for crimes they didn't commit"; while "the changing cast" – which has ranged from Gabriel Byrne to Richard Dreyfuss to Kathleen Turner – adds star quality, it's "an intense and moving piece of theater" whomever you watch.

90% Forbidden Broadway Ⓢ Ⓜ   22 | 19 | 19
Douglas Fairbanks, 432 W. 42nd St. (bet. 9th & 10th Aves.), 212-239-6200 (TC); www.forbiddenbroadway.com
With an ensemble cast; book & lyrics, Gerard Alessandrini; directors, Phillip George & Gerard Alessandrini.
■ "Broadway gets supremely spoofed through the rapid-fire parodies" of this long-running but "constantly updated"

revue that lovingly mocks musicals with new "deliciously clever" lyrics to familiar tunes; working with little more than a "bare-bones set", low-budget costumes and wigs, an "incredibly talented cast" delivers "spot-on send-ups of the Great White Way's denizens"; "you don't have to be an aficionado to appreciate the barbs", "but it's more fun if you are."

92% 42nd Street   22 | 19 | 26

Ford Center, 213 W. 42nd St. (bet. 7th & 8th Aves.), 212-307-4100 (TM); www.42ndstreetbroadway.com
With Beth Leavel & Tom Wopat; book, Mark Bramble & Michael Stewart; music, Harry Warren; lyrics, Al Dubin; director, Mark Bramble; choreographer, Randy Skinner.
■ "If you love old-fashioned musicals", "dance over to" the "beautifully restored" Ford Center for this "classic" of the genre, a "welcome revival" of the 1980 Gower Champion original (itself an adaptation of the 1933 film); a "true extravaganza" "jam-packed" with "razzle-dazzle", "lavish sets, phenomenal costumes" and Depression-era "hit songs", it's "comfort food for our troubled times"; sure, the "chorus-girl-becomes-a-star" plot "couldn't be cornier", but the storyline "is not the point" – this "vibrant, lively show" is all about "those tapping feet."

89% Golda's Balcony ⑤   27 | 24 | 24

Manhattan Ensemble, 55 Mercer St. (bet. Broome & Grand Sts.), 212-239-6200 (TC); www.met.com
With Tovah Feldshuh; by William Gibson; director, Scott Schwartz.
■ At a crisis point in the 1973 Yom Kippur war, Golda Meir ponders strategy – and by extension, her life – in this "powerful and timely" one-woman drama by William Gibson (*The Miracle Worker*); aided by "extremely effective" visual projections and some terrific makeup, a "magnificent" Tovah Feldshuh "really comes off" as the Prime Minister.

— Gypsy (Open 5/01) Ⓜ   – | – | –

Shubert, 225 W. 44th St. (bet. 7th & 8th Aves.), 212-239-6200 (TC); www.gypsythemusical.com
With Bernadette Peters, Tammy Blanchard & John Dossett; book, Arthur Laurents; music, Jule Styne; lyrics, Stephen Sondheim; director, Sam Mendes; choreographer, Jerome Robbins; additional choreography, Jerry Mitchell.
Ready or not, here comes mama!; based on the memoirs of legendary stripper Gypsy Rose Lee, this revival (previewing at press time) of one of the classic "textbook examples of what a musical should be" boasts "brilliant" Bernadette Peters (leading "a remarkable cast") as the ultimate stage mom obsessed with making her daughter a vaudeville star; Sam Mendes' "well-thought-out" staging preserves Jerome Robbins' original choreography, and that superb Styne–Sondheim score ('Everything's Coming Up Roses', 'Small World') is heard in its fully orchestrated glory.

95% **Hairspray**   27 | 24 | 28
Neil Simon, 250 W. 52nd St. (bet. B'way & 8th Ave.),
212-307-4100 (TM); www.hairsprayonbroadway.com
With Harvey Fierstein & Marissa Jaret Winokur; book,
Mark O'Donnell & Thomas Meehan; music, Marc Shaiman;
lyrics, Marc Shaiman & Scott Wittman; director, Jack
O'Brien; choreographer, Jerry Mitchell.
■ "Believe the hype": this "fresh" "feel-good musical"
"adaptation of [John Waters'] cult movie" about a 1960s
TV bandstand show is "as wonderful as everyone says"; it's
adorned with a "campy, candy-colored" "confection" of a
set, a "playful score" as "exhilarating" as white rain and a
"stellar" cast headed by the "superb Winokur" as "the
chunky girl who gets the hunky guy" while "breaking down
racial barriers"; however, the "phenomenal Fierstein"
"steals the show" in his "hysterical" yet "touching" "drag
role" that "oughta aqua-net him a trophy "come Tony time."

96% **Hank Williams: Lost Highway**   S 26 | 24 | 25
Little Shubert, 422 W. 42nd St. (bet. 9th & 10th Aves.),
212-239-6200 (TC); www.met.com
With Jason Petty; by Randal Myler & Mark Harelik;
music & lyrics, Hank Williams; director, Randal Myler.
■ "Even if you're not a country music fan, you'll end up
tapping your toes" at this "heartfelt" musical biography
of the Grand Ole Opry star, who died at age 29 in 1953;
"beautifully conceived" and chock-full of standards ('Your
Cheatin' Heart', 'Hey, Good-Lookin'), it "captures both the
essence of the period and the essence of Williams" – thanks
to "Jason Petty, who is just remarkable as Hank."

84% **I Love You, You're Perfect,**   20 | 20 | 18
Now Change S M
Westside, 407 W. 43rd St. (bet. 9th & 10th Aves.),
212-239-6200 (TC); www.loveperfectchange.com
With Frank Baiocchi, Jordan Leeds, Janet Metz & Karyn
Quackenbush; book & lyrics, Joe DiPietro; music, Jimmy
Roberts; director, Joel Bishoff.
■ A "comedic romp through relationships" between men
and women "at different stages", this long-running musical
revue makes for a good "date show", with "cute songs" and
"clever skits" – even if they skate close to "stereotypical";
as the "talented cast of four" "zings couples of all ages",
you'll "enjoy laughing at them, and ultimately at yourself."

88% **La Bohème**   23 | 24 | 26
Broadway, 1681 Broadway (bet. 52nd & 53rd Sts.),
212-239-6200 (TC); www.bohemeonbroadway.com
With alternating principal casts; composer, Giacomo
Puccini; libretto, Giuseppe Giacosa & Luigi Illica; director,
Baz Luhrmann.
■ *Moulin Rouge* director "Baz Luhrmann brings opera to
the masses" in this busy mounting of Puccini's masterpiece,

updated to 1957 Paris with "free-wheeling" subtitles and a "va-va-voomy cast" to portray the starving yet starry-eyed bohemian artists; though the "rotating" principals "can actually act" as well as sing those "can't-be-beat arias", Catherine Martin's "mesmerizing" "sets nearly steal the show"; of course, "true aficionados will be disappointed by the diminished orchestra and use of body mikes", but the majority melts over "the most moving musical in town."

75% **Last Sunday in June** ⑤   ▽ 21 | 18 | 20
Century Center for the Performing Arts, 111 E. 15th St. (bet. Irving Plaza & Union Sq. E.), 212-239-6200 (TC); www.rattlestick.org
With Johnathan F. McClain & Peter Smith; by Jonathan Tolins; director, Trip Cullman.
☑ As a young male couple watches the annual Gay Pride Parade from their Christopher Street apartment, assorted friends, past and present, drop by, leading to happy, sad and rueful revelations on the universal themes of fidelity, careers and even marriage to a woman; this "well-acted and -directed" comedy-drama both parodies and celebrates the notion of the 'gay play', causing converts to call it "a *Boys in the Band* for the new century", even if a divergent quarter disses "a few too many self-referential jokes."

86% **Late Night Catechism**   22 | 19 | 17
St. Luke's Church, 308 W. 46th St. (bet. 8th & 9th Aves), 212-239-6200 (TC); www.latenitecatechism.com
With Colleen O'Neill; by Maripat Donovan & Vicki Quade; director, Patrick Trettenero.
■ Though "people who went to parochial school will appreciate it" the most, "you don't have to be Catholic" to enjoy this long-running re-creation of religious remedial education at the hands of a stern Sister who, by treating the audience as students, makes "even Jews" "feel like they're in a classroom" ("having it in a church basement is a nice touch"); just "don't arrive late, otherwise you will get yelled at"; N.B. Saturday and Sunday only.

93% **Les Misérables**   25 | 26 | 27
Imperial, 249 W. 45th St. (bet. B'way & 8th Ave.), 212-239-6200 (TC); www.lesmis.com
With Randal Keith, Jayne Paterson, Michael McCarthy & Diana Kaarina; book, Alain Boublil & Claude-Michel Schönberg; music, Claude-Michel Schönberg; lyrics, Herbert Kretzmer; director, Trevor Nunn & John Caird.
■ It's scheduled to run until May 18 and not 'One Day More', so hurry if you don't want to miz this "five-hanky", three-hour "tour de force" that many call their "favorite musical of all time"; "following the classic novel" by Victor Hugo about the reformed prisoner Jean Valjean and the puritanical Inspector Javert, it's "a 19th-century melodrama brought to the stage with the best 20th-century imagination" – e.g.

"spectacular scenery" (including that "famed turntable")
and "special musical numbers"; the cast generally raises
"amazing voices" in a "heartrending" score that ranges
from "tender to stirring."

69% Life (x) 3   25 | 16 | 21

Circle in the Square, 1633 Broadway (bet. 50th & 51st Sts.),
212-239-6200 (TC)
With Helen Hunt, John Turturro, Linda Emond & Brent Spiner;
by Yazmina Reza; translation, Christopher Hampton;
director, Matthew Warchus.
◪ "The same story" – a husband and wife arrive at another
couple's home for dinner on the wrong night – "is presented
several times, each with a different slant" in this "superbly
performed" new work by Yasmina Reza (who penned the
1998 Tony Award winner *Art* as well as *The Unexpected
Man*) that "takes you from outright laughter to pondering
your own existence in the universe"; some wonder "what's
the point?" but most feel each of the "three variations
hits home", as does "Act 4: after you leave, you'll keep
talking about it for days."

94% Lion King, The   23 | 22 | 29

New Amsterdam, 214 W. 42nd St. (bet. 7th & 8th Aves.),
212-307-4100 (TM); disney.go.com
*With Clifton Oliver, Derek Smith & Samuel E. Wright; book,
Roger Allers & Irene Mecchi; music, Elton John; lyrics, Tim
Rice; director, Julie Taymor; choreographer, Garth Fagan.*
■ "A brilliant re-conceptualization of the Disney movie
musical, transporting you to a magical land", this "visual
feast" remains "great for the entire family", even after
ruling – er, running – for five years; director/costume
designer Julie Taymor is a "genius who redefines theater
for the 21st century", with "animals that come to life in her
giant puppet creations", "awe-inspiring scenery" by Richard
Hudson and "unforgettable music" and dancing; a few
growl over the "lame jokes" and "*Hamlet*-lite plot" about a
lion cub's coming-of-age, but the near-unanimous majority
lionizes it as "definitely something to roar about."

— Look of Love, The (Open 5/04)   _ | _ | _

Brooks Atkinson, 256 W. 47th St. (bet. B'way & 8th Aves.),
212-307-4100 (TM); www.lookofloveonbroadway.com
*With an ensemble cast; music, Burt Bacharach; lyrics, Hal
David; director, Scott Ellis; choreographer, Ann Reinking.*
Previewing at press time, this nine-person musical revue
from the Roundabout Theatre Company intends to prove
that What the World Needs Now is a retrospective of some
30 smooth-as-silk songs by Burt Bacharach and Hal David;
ranging from 'Alfie' to 'Promises, Promises' (from the
team's sole Broadway show), this "delightful showcase"
also features "some lively dancing" choreographed by
Ann Reinking, of *Chicago* and *Fosse* fame.

87% **Mamma Mia!**   22 | 17 | 24

Cadillac Winter Garden, 1634 Broadway (bet. 50th & 51st Sts.),
212-563-5544 (TC); www.mamma-mia.com
*With Lousie Pitre, Tina Maddigan & David W. Keeley; book,
Catherine Johnson; music & lyrics, Benny Andersson &
Björn Ulvaeus; director, Phyllida Lloyd; choreographer,
Anthony van Laast.*
■ "ABBA-cadabra!" show-goers in search of "pure
unadulterated fun, with no thought required", should
"definitely take a chance on this show", based on the
1970s Swedish group Abba's "contagious" disco hits; sure,
the "paper-thin plot" has to "do complicated yoga moves
to incorporate the songs" ("heavily miked with apparently
little change from the albums' scoring"), but the "cast
exudes high energy", particularly "petite powerhouse
Louise Pitre" as the mother of a bride-to-be; by the "rousing"
"mini-concert at the end", everyone will be "boogying up
the aisles" "like a dancing queen or king."

86% **Man of La Mancha**   24 | 23 | 23

Martin Beck, 302 W. 45th St. (bet. 8th & 9th Aves.),
212-239-6200 (TC); www.manoflamancha.com
*With Brian Stokes Mitchell, Mary Elizabeth Mastrantonio &
Ernie Sabella; book, Dale Wasserman; music, Mitch Leigh;
lyrics, Joe Darion; director, Jonathan Kent; choreographer,
Luis Perez.*
◪ Don Quixote rides again in this latest remounting of
the musical based on Cervantes' "man vs. windmill"
masterpiece; it remains "a theatrical coup", thanks to its
"truly inspiring story" and "memorable score" including,
of course, 'The Impossible Dream' – "Brian Stokes Mitchell's
soaring baritone rendition" of which "alone is worth
the price of admission"; an unchivalrous flock finds the
"supporting cast mediocre" and the set "overblown"
(especially compared with the 1965 original), but the
majority dubs this a "good, solid revival of a classic."

91% **Menopause The Musical**   22 | 22 | 21

Playhouse 91, 316 E. 91st St. (bet. 1st & 2nd Aves.),
212-831-2000 (BO); www.menopausethemusical.com
*With Lynn Eldredge, Joy Lynn Matthews, Carolann Page & Sally
Ann Swarm; by Jeanie Linders; director, Kathleen Lindsey.*
■ "Great fun for a girls' night out" is the diagnosis for
this loosely constructed musical about four menopausal
ladies, "a cross-section of female America", who bond in
Bloomingdale's; "every post-childbearing woman should
see this to have a good laugh" at the "parodies of pop
standards" – 'Change of Life' to the tune of 'Chain of Fools',
'Staying Awake' in place of 'Staying Alive', etc.; "as the
name suggests, it reaches out to a narrow audience"
(though actually, "even some husbands like it"), but the
high recommendation levels indicate this show is no hot-
flash-in-the-pan.

75% **Movin' Out** 20 15 23
Richard Rodgers, 226 W. 46th St. (bet. B'way & 8th Ave.),
212-307-4100 (TM); www.movinoutonbroadway.com
With Michael Cavanaugh, Elizabeth Parkinson, Keith Roberts,
John Selya & Ashley Tuttle; music & lyrics, Billy Joel;
choreographer & director, Twyla Tharp.
☑ "Telling a story solely through the music and lyrics of
Billy Joel isn't easy, but Twyla Tharp manages to pull it off"
profess fans of this "frequently gripping" "dance-drama
about young people during the Vietnam era"; skeptics
scold that "with no dialogue", the "plot seems thinner than
the air atop Mt. Everest" and recoil at the "rock-concert
pitch"; however, "despite some missteps", most deem the
piece "moving, in both senses of the word"; P.S. the savvy
say "be sure to see it with Michael Cavanaugh", who
"sings the entire score", and the primary cast of "sublime"
American Ballet Theatre principals.

63% **Murdered by The Mob** 14 14 14
Arno Ristorante, 141 W. 38th St. (bet. B'way & 7th Ave.),
800-687-3374 (BO); www.murdermysteryinc.com
With an ensemble cast; by Joni Pacie; director, Ron Pacie.
☑ Now in its seventh year, this interactive murder mystery
is obviously a hit by any definition; challenging audiences
to guess who whacked whom, the "stereotypical" "mob-
inspired" antics are "funny and worth seeing" giggle good-
hearted fellas; but while dinner and dancing are included
in the price, wiseguys advise "eat before or after the
show" – and one-third of those surveyed would prefer to
cop out entirely; N.B. Friday and Saturday nights only.

78% **Naked Boys Singing!** S M 17 13 17
Actors' Playhouse, 100 Seventh Ave. S. (bet. Bleecker &
W. 4th Sts.), 212-239-6200 (TC); www.nakedboysinging.com
With an ensemble cast; conceived & directed by Robert
Schrock; choreographer, Jeffry Denman.
☑ Yes, "they sure are" in this long-running musical revue
that "delivers what it advertises" – eight "bare boys who
warble winsomely", performing numbers that celebrate
their members; whether "you're a gay man or a woman
with a bachelorette party", one thing's for sure – "you
won't take your eyes off this stage", even if a few skeptics
shrug that "once the novelty wears off", the acting and
"so-so songs" "leave much to be desired."

88% **Nine** 26 20 24
Eugene O'Neill, 230 W. 49th St. (bet. B'way & 8th Ave.),
212-239-6200 (TC); www.nineonbroadway.com
With Antonio Banderas, Laura Benanti, Jane Krakowski,
Mary Stuart Masterson & Chita Rivera; book, Arthur Kopit;
music & lyrics, Maury Yeston; director, David Leveaux.
■ An "exceptional cast" enlivens the first Broadway revival
of the 1982 hit, an "inspired" if "distant" musical version of

the Fellini film *8½*; as the show's sole adult male, lead "Antonio Banderas is a revelation", playing a director on the verge of a nervous breakdown; among the numerous women in his life, show-goers single out "fabulous, sexy" Jane Krakowski and Chita Rivera ("46 years after *West Side Story*", she "still has it!"); with almost nine out of ten reviewers recommending it, small wonder its limited run just got extended.

81% **Our Lady of 121st Street** S   25 │ 18 │ 20
Union Square, 100 E. 17th St. (bet. Irving Plaza & Union Square E.), 212-307-4100 (TM); www.ourlady121.com
With an ensemble cast; by Stephen Adly Guirgis; director, Philip Seymour Hoffman.
◪ Thanks to "riveting acting", this "in-your-face drama" about a group of childhood friends reunited at a beloved nun's funeral manages to be "intensely comic and tragic at the same time"; but while its coterie of converts contends the "confrontational scenes are terrific", plot-oriented purists insist "they don't add up to a play" – "just a variety show of epiphany and rage."

36% **Perfect Crime** S M   12 │ 11 │ 11
Duffy, 1553 Broadway (bet. 46th & 47th Sts.), 212-695-3401 (BO); www.perfect-crime.com
With Catharine Russell, David Butler, Michael Minor & Charles Geyer; by Warren Manzi; director, Jeffrey Hyatt.
◪ "With every minute, the plot gets weirder" in this "long-, long-, long-running murder mystery" ("*The Mousetrap* of NYC"), "located in a room above a store in Times Square"; though to some it's "a classic little whodunit" – "nothing deep, just fun and enjoyable" – two-thirds of surveyors find it "more ghastly than ghostly" and bristle at the "low-budget" digs (it gets "depressing" "sitting in folding chairs"); some suggest that the perfect crime is what they manage to perform at the box office.

88% **Phantom of the Opera, The** M   23 │ 23 │ 26
Majestic, 247 W. 44th St. (bet. 7th & 8th Aves.), 212-239-6200 (TC); www.thephantomoftheopera.com
With Hugh Panaro & Lisa Vroman; book, Andrew Lloyd Webber & Richard Stilgoe; music, Andrew Lloyd Webber; lyrics, Charles Hart & Richard Stilgoe; director, Harold Prince; choreographer, Gillian Lynne.
■ "Still casts its spell" marvel myriad musical-goers "mesmerized" by this long-running Andrew Lloyd Webber "blockbuster", a "smoke-and-mirrors"–filled "masquerade of beautiful costumes", "dazzling sets" and special effects that are so "spectacular" they "could have a [hit] without any actors or story"; still, the performers' "voices are marvelous" as they sing the "haunting" score and enact the tale of a mysterious figure smitten by a young opera singer in 19th-century Paris; so if your visitors (or you)

want to see a bit of "classic B'way", definitely "pay the phantom a visit."

75% Play What I Wrote, The   23 | 15 | 20
Lyceum, 149 W. 45th St. (bet. 6th & 7th Aves.), 212-239-6200 (TC); www.playwhatiwrote.com
With Sean Foley, Hamish McColl, Toby Jones & Mystery Guest; by Hamish McColl, Sean Foley & Eddie Braben; music & lyrics, Gary Yershon; director, Kenneth Branagh.
■ "Impeccable timing, a few vulgar physical jokes and excruciating wordplay" – in short, the "crème de la crème of British music hall comedy" – are on display in this "fast-paced" "little import from across the pond"; the story (such as it is) involves the efforts of one member of a comic duo to mount a play he's written for a big star; the "great gimmick" is that every few days, a different surprise guest (participants have included Kevin Kline, Roger Moore and Liam Neeson) actually appears as himself to join the "energetically manic cast" in "calculated silliness."

95% Producers, The   26 | 26 | 27
St. James, 246 W. 44th St. (bet. 7th & 8th Aves.), 212-239-5800 (TC); www.producersonbroadway.com
With Lewis J. Stadlin & Don Stephenson; book, Mel Brooks & Thomas Meehan; music & lyrics, Mel Brooks; directed & choreographed by Susan Stroman.
■ You're guaranteed "a gag a minute" at this "good old-fashioned" "zany musical", which swept the 2001 Tony Awards; based on the "classic Mel Brooks film" about two "brilliantly stupid" get-rich-quicksters' scheme to produce a surefire flop entitled *Springtime for Hitler* and pocket their investors' funds, it offers "lavish production numbers", "songs you'll hum afterward" and a "joke-saturated" book that boasts "something to offend everyone"; although original leads Nathan Lane and Matthew Broderick are sorely "missed", most reviewers report the "new cast is still great fun."

80% Rent S M   22 | 22 | 22
Nederlander, 208 W. 41st St. (bet. 7th & 8th Aves.), 212-307-4100 (TM); www.siteforrent.com
With an ensemble cast; book, music & lyrics, Jonathan Larson; director, Michael Greif.
☑ "Especially poignant in light of composer Larson's shortened life", this "emotional", "edgy" rock musical "adapts *La Bohème* to modern-day NYC", depicting twentysomething artists "trying to survive on nothing more than their aspirations"; would-be bohemians call it "an Alphabet City classic", with "superb statements regarding gays, HIV and discrimination"; but establishment types are ready to evict, saying that while still "heartfelt", the show seems "a little dated now" and definitely "over-amplified" ("ok, I cried, but maybe because my ears hurt").

91% Rhapsody in Seth ⑤   ▽ 23 | 23 | 21

Actors' Playhouse, 100 Seventh Ave. S. (bet. Bleecker &
W. 4th Sts.), 212-239-6200 (TC); www.rhapsodyinseth.com
Written and performed by Seth Rudetsky; director, Peter Flynn.
■ Conductor, benefits producer, comedy writer (credits
include *The Rosie O'Donnell Show*) and all-around "neat
guy" Seth Rudetsky "speaks for underdogs everywhere"
in his "autobiographical" "one-man show" that describes
being "a gay teenager in love with musicals" on Long
Island, along with an "insider's take on the best of B'way";
his "great good humor and first-rate musicianship" make
for an "extremely witty" evening.

82% Russell Simmons'   23 | 18 | 20
    Def Poetry Jam ⑤

Longacre, 220 W. 48th St. (bet. B'way & 8th Ave.),
212-239-6200 (TC); www.defpoetryjamnyc.com
With an ensemble cast; created by Stan Lathan & Russell
Simmons; music, DJ Tendaji; director, Stan Lathan.
◪ "Refreshing, vibrant" and "full of street smarts", this
"valiant effort to present slam poetry to the masses"
features nine "passionate young voices" (plus a DJ) "from a
rich tapestry of ethnic backgrounds" offering alternately
"joyful" and "controversial", "evocative and disturbing"
observations about contemporary life that will "leave you
in awe of the power of the spoken word"; while the set's
"nothing elaborate" and the material's "too angry" for the
easily offended, it's got "enough energy to light up the
Great White Way."

— **Salome** (Open 4/30) Ⓜ   ⌐|⌐|⌐

Ethel Barrymore, 243 W. 47th St. (bet. Broadway & 8th Ave.),
212-239-6200 (TC); www.salomeonbroadway.com
With Al Pacino, Marisa Tomei, Dianne Wiest & David
Strathairn; by Oscar Wilde; original music, Yukio Tsuji;
director, Estelle Parsons.
Handling "drama and comedy with equal aplomb", Al
Pacino plays the lustful King Herod and a "captivating"
Marisa Tomei his strip-teasing step-daughter in this "early
Oscar Wilde" work that "seductively" retells the biblical
story of John the Baptist's death; though technically 'a
reading' (the actors sometimes carry scripts and the
production is bare-bones), the "stellar cast" and director
Estelle Parsons' "intense" staging "make it real" say
surveyors who saw previews.

93% Say Goodnight Gracie: 27 | 23 | 21
    The Love, Laughter and Life of George Burns

Helen Hayes, 240 W. 44th St. (bet. 7th & 8th Aves.),
212-239-6200 (TC); www.saygoodnightgracie.net
With Frank Gorshin; by Rupert Holmes; director, John Tillinger.
■ "Frank Gorshin is George Burns reincarnated" in this
"well-conceived one-man show" that has the late performer

reviewing his life so he can reunite with wife and comedy partner Gracie Allen in heaven; using "film clips as context", it's a trip down "memory lane", "a love story and a fantasy all rolled into one", anchored by the actor's "incredible impersonation"; and if unabashedly "for the nostalgia crowd" ('Gracie who?' ask audience members under 40), it's still a "lovely and very touching tribute" to a beloved and "inseparable couple."

85% **Stomp** S   18 | 13 | 23

Orpheum, 126 Second Ave. (bet. 7th & 8th Sts.), 212-477-2477 (BO); www.stomponline.com
With an ensemble cast; created & directed by Luke Cresswell & Steve McNicholas.
◪ "You'll be finger-tapping and fork-clanking for weeks" after taking in this "original and cool" wordless revue in which "wonderfully talented" "performers make music with average everyday objects"; a long-running East Village fixture, its "combination of percussion, acrobatics, dance and comedy" "makes houseguests feel hip", is "great for kids" and "simply amazing for anyone who possesses rhythm"; however, "bring earplugs" and Excedrin and "sit in the back" or else "you'll feel like it's your brain that's been stomped."

91% **Take Me Out**   26 | 23 | 25

Walter Kerr, 219 W. 48th St. (bet. B'way & 8th Ave.), 212-239-6200 (TC)
With Daniel Sunjata & Denis O'Hare; by Richard Greenberg; director, Joe Mantello.
■ A "gay baseball player comes out of the closet" and his teammates go into shock in this "original" "meditation on American culture", a "risky, thought-provoking" play with "brilliant monologues", an "imaginative" locker-room setting and "spot-on performances" (notably from the "show-stealing Denis O'Hare"); overall, it's a "home run", though its notorious "full-frontal" shower scenes where the "buff" cast "lets it all hang out" lead some to suggest it for "mature audiences" only.

92% **Talking Heads** S   ▽ 26 | 24 | 21

Minetta Lane, 18 Minetta Ln. (bet. MacDougal St. & 6th Ave.), 212-307-4100 (TM); www.talkingheadsoffbroadway.com
With alternating casts; by Alan Bennett; director, Michael Engler.
■ For "subtle British wit at its best" – and "terrific acting" by Kathleen Chalfant, Daniel Davis, Lynn Redgrave and Frances Sternhagen – theatergoers talk up this offering from playwright Alan Bennett (*The Madness of King George*); it's actually not a single play, but seven separate soliloquies, performed in alternating programs that are unrelated – except that each monologue "poignantly" and "engagingly tells" of a lonely individual who experiences a life-altering twist of fate.

89% **Tea at Five**   27 | 18 | 21

Promenade, 2162 Broadway (bet. 76th & 77th Sts.),
212-239-6200 (TC); www.teaat5.com
*With Kate Mulgrew; by Matthew Lombardo; director,
John Tillinger.*
☑ "Kate (Mulgrew) does Kate (Hepburn)" in this "classy"
one-woman show, a "famous-person impersonation" that
"marvelously" unfolds in two acts (set in 1938 and 1983);
maybe the "story lacks real insight" and "never delves too
deep", but hold out for the "perfect second act" when the
"wig, costume" and "fiery" performance nails the older
actress "to a 'tea'" say the nine out of ten theatergoers
who'd recommend this to their friends.

87% **Thoroughly Modern Millie**   24 | 20 | 25

Marquis, 1535 Broadway (bet. 46th & 47th Sts.),
212-307-4100 (TM); www.modernmillie.com
*With Sutton Foster & Harriet Harris; book, Richard Morris
& Dick Scanlan; new music, Jeanine Tesori; new lyrics,
Dick Scanlan; director, Michael Mayer.*
■ "Fun, frothy" and "light as a feather", this "throwback to
more innocent times" "in the grand Broadway musical
tradition" stars "gangly, gorgeous Sutton Foster" as a
"small-town girl who takes NY by storm in the '20s"; though
the "silly storyline" and "politically incorrect" "white-slavery
subplot" are "not so modern", there are enough "rousing",
"well-danced" numbers (especially that "typewriter scene")
to make it a "great getaway" that leaves "a huge smile on
every audience member's face."

77% **Tony N' Tina's Wedding** S   17 | 17 | 18

St. Luke's Church, 308 W. 46th St. (bet. 8th & 9th Aves.),
212-354-0161 (BO); www.tonylovestina.com
*With Joli Tribuzio & Scott Billocky; created by the Artificial
Intelligence troupe; director, Larry Pellegrini.*
☑ "An irreverent take on the ultimate bad Italian wedding",
this comedy makes you "join the cast for the hilarious"
nuptials, so "only go if you like audience participation"
(there's a dinner reception too though most predict the
"limp pasta" "would get panned in *Zagat NYC Restaurants*");
sure, it's "silly", but the fact that it's hung around "all these
years" ("they've been married more times than Liz Taylor")
proves it's "entertaining"; N.B. final vows are set for May 18.

46% **Urban Cowboy** M   14 | 10 | 15

Broadhurst, 235 W. 44th St. (bet. 7th & 8th Aves.),
212-239-6200 (TC); www.urbancowboythemusical.com
*With Matt Cavenaugh & Jenn Colella; book, Aaron Latham
& Phillip Oesterman; new music & lyrics, Jason Robert
Brown & Jeff Blumenkrantz; director, Lonny Price;
choreographer, Melinda Roy.*
☑ Even the 1980 film hit's original popular country songs,
plus some "decent" new ones by composers Jason Robert

Brown (who leads the omnipresent onstage band) and Jeff Blumenkrantz, can't corral this new musical's "hokey" story, about young wanna-be cowboys and cowgirls who hang out at a Houston singles bar; as to the show's other elements, pals praise the "energetic" performances and "foot-stomping choreography" as "fun, Texas-style"; but more urbane types find the focus on "the leading man's abs" and displays of machismo "as mechanical as the mechanical bull" that the characters ride.

81% Urinetown: The Musical　　24 | 21 | 22

Henry Miller's, 124 W. 43rd St. (bet. B'way & 6th Ave.), 212-239-6200 (TC); www.urinetown.com

With John Cullum, Charlie Pollock & Jennifer Laura Thompson; book, Greg Kotis; music & lyrics, Mark Hollmann & Greg Kotis; director, John Rando.

◪ "Look past the title to be entertained" by this "quirky Brechtian musical", a "dark tinkle of a tale" about a "drought-stricken" "world where you have to pay to pee"; though it "mocks the whole genre", supporters smile it's "solidly constructed", with a "rich score and witty writing" (if a bit "irritatingly smug" say some); even cynics who snap the "stylized joke" "is stretched out too long" admit that the "phenomenal cast saves" it; P.S. "there's no charge for using the theater's restrooms."

82% Women of Lockerbie, The　　▽ 24 | 23 | 22

Theatre at St. Clement's, 423 W. 46th St. (bet. 9th & 10th Aves.), 212-279-4200 (TS); www.thenewgroup.org

With Judith Ivey & Larry Pine; by Deborah Brevoort; director, Wilson Milam.

■ It's 1995, and a couple whose son died on Pan Am Flight 103 journey to Lockerbie, Scotland, to find closure in this new "powerful piece", done in the style of a "Greek tragedy (chorus included)"; with the action unfolding in the course of one night, it's a "heavy subject, but handled beautifully", on a simple set of wooden stairs, with performances that "strike chords of recognition"; N.B. the play derives its title from real-life women of the town, who collected and returned the victims' clothes — sorted, washed and neatly packed — to surviving family members.

94% Year With Frog and Toad, A 🆂　▽ 24 | 21 | 24

Cort, 138 W. 48th St. (bet. 6th & 7th Aves.), 212-239-6200 (TC); www.frogandtoadonbroadway.com

With Mark Linn-Baker & Jay Goede; book, Willie Reale; music, Robert Reale; lyrics, Willie Reale; director, David Petrarca.

■ There ain't "no flies on this production" about two amphibian best friends, based on the children's stories of Arnold Lobel and produced and set-designed by his daughter Adrianne; intimate and "irony-free", it's a "fun family romp" (for ages four and up) as it "colorfully" chronicles the musical adventures of Frog (Jay Goede) and Toad (Mark Linn-Baker, aka Mr. Adrianne Lobel) through one calendar year, encountering various critters and learning about relationships as they go.

87% **Zanna, Don't!** 🅂   23 | 20 | 22

John Houseman, 450 W. 42nd St. (bet. 9th & 10th Aves.), 212-239-6200 (TC); www.zannadont.com
With Jai Rodriguez; book, music & lyrics, Tim Acito; directed & choreographed by Devanand Janki.
■ Set in an "upside-down world" – a high school where homosexuals predominate, making heterosexuals the divergent minority – this "spoofy, upbeat take on straight-gay relationships" charms with a "fabulously" lively pop-rock score, "terrific ensemble cast" and "creative staging" on brightly colored, if low-tech, sets; though admittedly "fluffy", it manages to be "uplifting and touching" too – so zophisticated supporters say "Zanna, do" keep on singing.

Theater Seating Charts

Ambassador

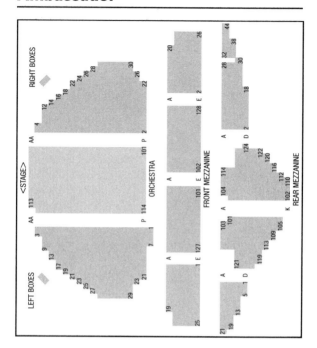

American Airlines

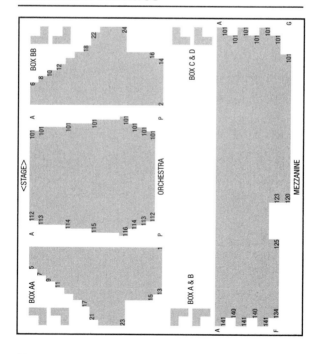

subscribe to zagat.com

Belasco

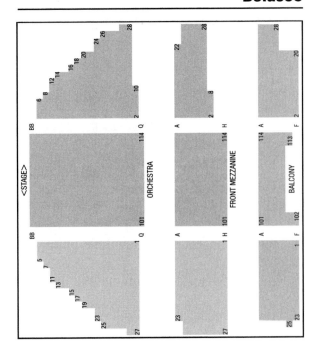

STAGE

ORCHESTRA

FRONT MEZZANINE

BALCONY

Broadhurst

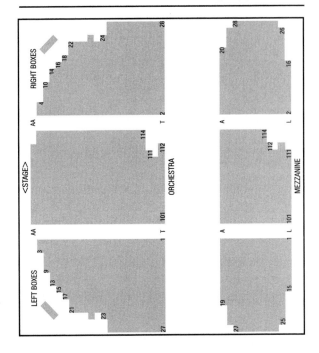

STAGE

RIGHT BOXES

LEFT BOXES

ORCHESTRA

MEZZANINE

Broadway

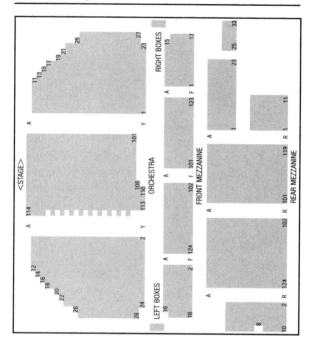

Brooks Atkinson

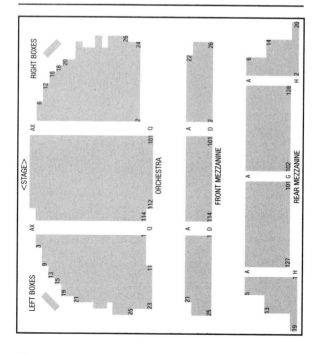

Cadillac Winter Garden

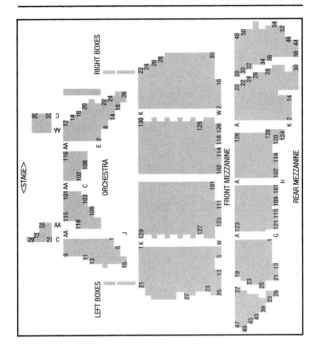

Circle in the Square

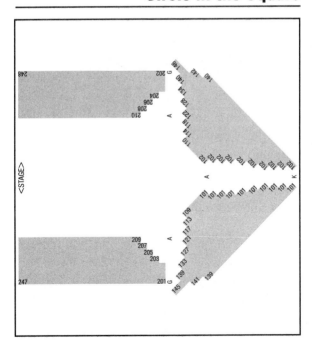

Cort

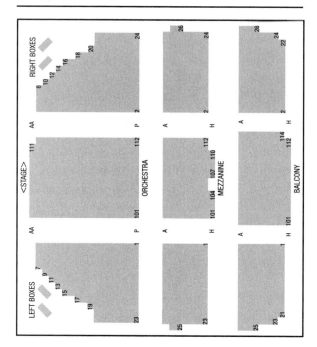

Ethel Barrymore

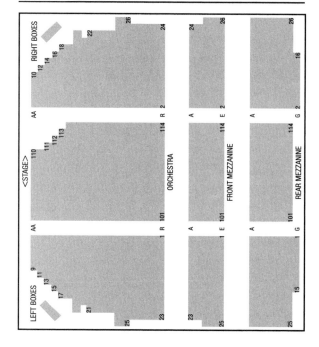

Eugene O'Neill

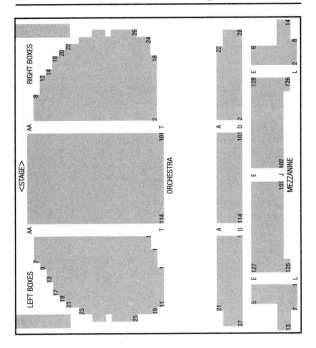

Ford Center for the Performing Arts

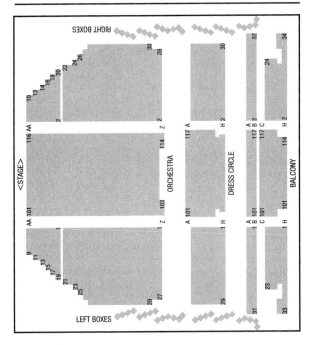

Helen Hayes

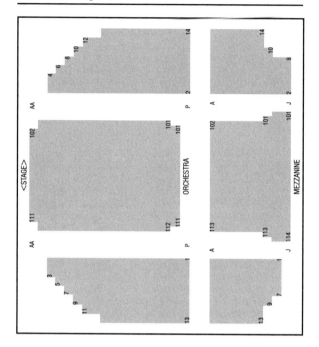

Henry Miller's

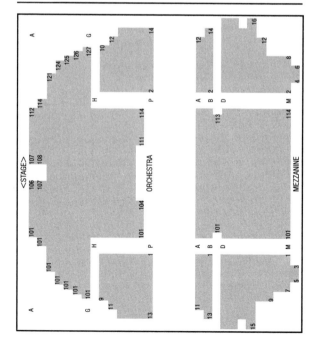

Imperial

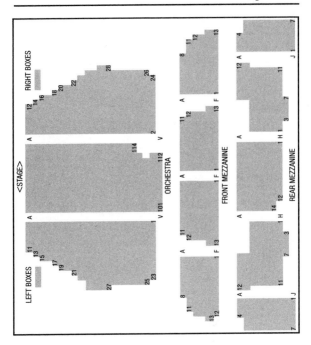

RIGHT BOXES

LEFT BOXES

<STAGE>

ORCHESTRA

FRONT MEZZANINE

REAR MEZZANINE

John Golden

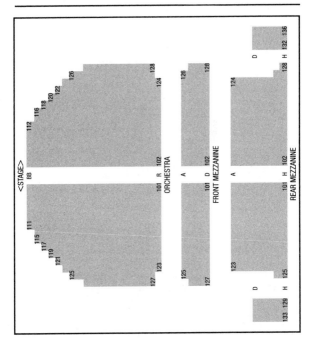

<STAGE>

ORCHESTRA

FRONT MEZZANINE

REAR MEZZANINE

Lamb's Theater

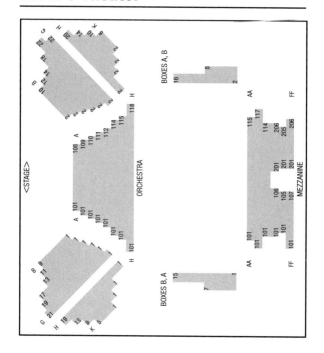

Longacre

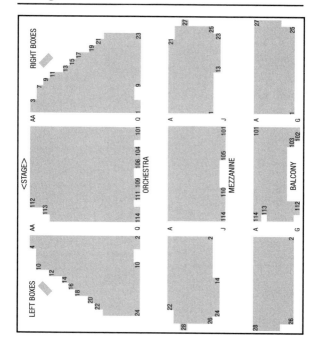

subscribe to zagat.com

Lunt-Fontanne

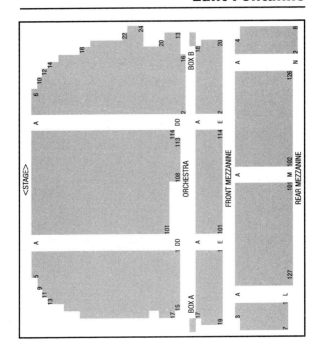

Lyceum

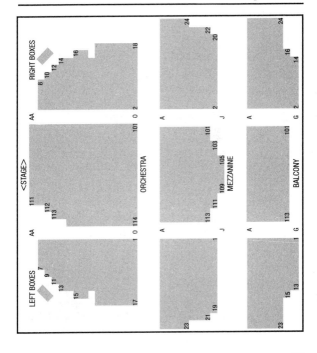

Majestic

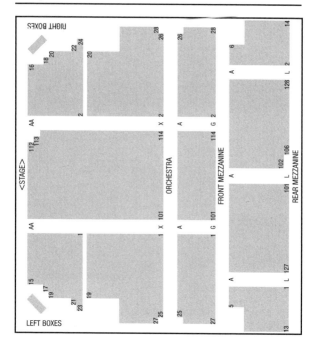

Marquis

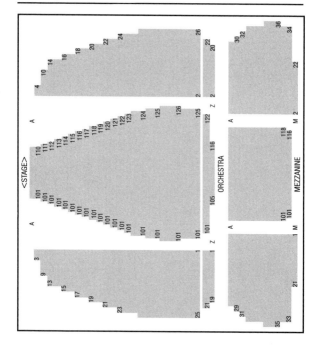

subscribe to zagat.com

Martin Beck

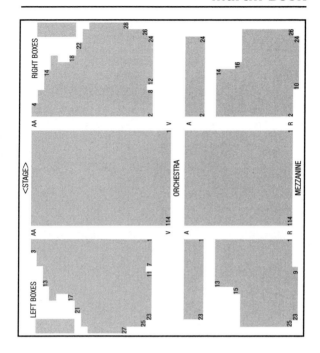

Nederlander

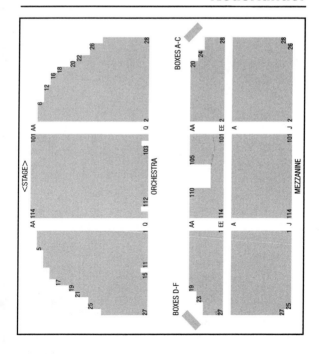

Neil Simon

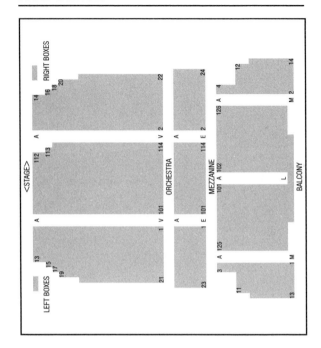

New Amsterdam

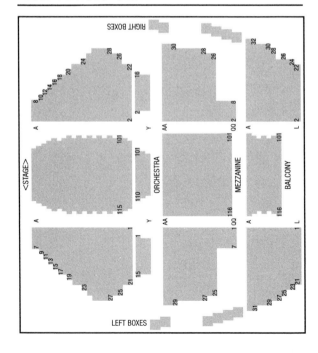

Palace

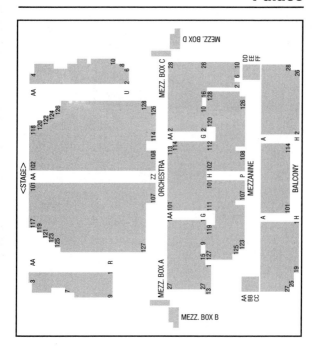

Richard Rodgers

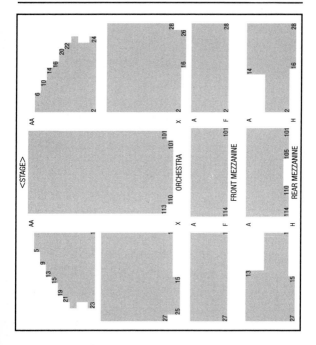

Shubert

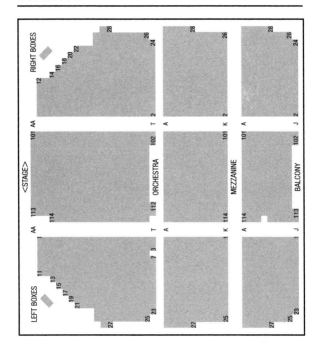

St. James

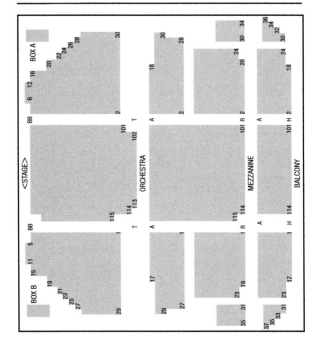

Studio 54

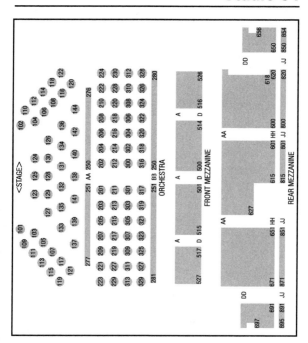

Walter Kerr

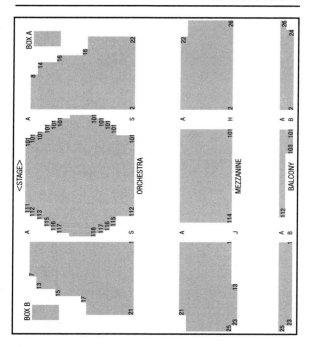

Theater Indexes

GENRES
LOCATIONS
SPECIAL FEATURES

Indexes list the best of many within each category.

GENRES

Comedies
Barbra's Wedding
Enchanted April
Last Sunday
Life (x) 3
Murder by Mob
Play I Wrote
Say G'dnight Gracie
Tony N' Tina's

Dramas
Exonerated
Golda's Balcony
Joe Egg
Our Lady 121 St.
Perfect Crime
Salome
Take Me Out
Tea at Five
Women of Lockerbie

Musicals
Aida
Avenue Q
Beauty & Beast
Cabaret
Chicago
42nd Street
Gypsy
Hairspray
Hank Williams
La Bohème
Les Mis
Lion King
Mamma Mia
Man of La Mancha
Menopause
Movin' Out
Nine
Phantom of Opera
Producers
Rent
Thoroughly MM
Urban Cowboy
Urinetown
Year With Frog...
Zanna, Don't!

Performance Works
Blue Man Group
Def Poetry Jam
Donkey Show
Late Night Cat.
Stomp
Talking Heads

Revues
Dream a Little
Forbidden B'way
I Love You...
Look of Love
Naked Boys

Solo Shows
As Long as We Laugh
Down Long Road
Rhapsody in Seth

LOCATIONS

Broadway
Aida
As Long as We Laugh
Beauty & Beast
Cabaret
Chicago
Def Poetry Jam
Enchanted April
42nd Street
Gypsy
Hairspray
Joe Egg
La Bohème
Les Mis
Life (x) 3
Lion King
Look of Love
Mamma Mia
Man of La Mancha
Movin' Out
Nine
Phantom of Opera
Play I Wrote
Producers
Rent
Salome
Say G'dnight Gracie
Take Me Out
Thoroughly MM
Urban Cowboy

Urinetown
Year With Frog...

Off-Broadway
Avenue Q
Barbra's Wedding
Blue Man Group
Donkey Show
Down Long Road
Dream a Little
Exonerated
Forbidden B'way
Golda's Balcony
Hank Williams
I Love You...
Last Sunday
Late Night Cat.
Menopause
Murder by Mob
Naked Boys
Our Lady 121 St.
Perfect Crime
Rhapsody in Seth
Stomp
Talking Heads
Tea at Five
Tony N' Tina's
Women of Lockerbie
Zanna, Don't!

SPECIAL FEATURES

Big Dance Numbers
Aida
Beauty & Beast
Cabaret
Chicago
42nd Street
Hairspray
Lion King
Mamma Mia
Movin' Out
Producers
Thoroughly MM
Urban Cowboy

Big-Name Choreographers
Cabaret, *Rob Marshall*
Chicago, *Ann Reinking*
Gypsy, *Jerome Robbins*
Look of Love, *Ann Reinking*
Movin' Out, *Twyla Tharp*
Producers, *Susan Stroman*

Big-Name Directors
Cabaret, *Sam Mendes*
Gypsy, *Sam Mendes*
La Bohème, *Baz Luhrmann*
Les Mis, *Trevor Nunn & John Caird*
Lion King, *Julie Taymor*
Movin' Out, *Twyla Tharp*
Our Lady 121 St., *Philip Seymour Hoffman*
Phantom of Opera, *Harold Prince*
Play I Wrote, *Kenneth Branagh*
Producers, *Susan Stroman*

Classics
La Bohème
Salome

Family Appeal
Beauty & Beast
Blue Man Group
42nd Street
Hairspray
Lion King
Stomp
Thoroughly MM
Year With Frog...

Imports
Cabaret
Joe Egg
Les Mis
Life (x) 3
Mamma Mia
Phantom of Opera
Play I Wrote
Stomp
Take Me Out

Limited Runs
As Long as We Laugh
Golda's Balcony
Joe Egg
Life (x) 3
Look of Love
Nine
Salome
Women of Lockerbie

Long-Running
(Two years or more)
Aida
Beauty & Beast
Blue Man Group
Cabaret
Chicago
Donkey Show
42nd Street
I Love You...
Late Night Cat.
Les Mis
Lion King
Murder by Mob
Naked Boys
Perfect Crime
Phantom of Opera
Producers
Rent
Stomp
Tony N' Tina's

Mature Audiences
Avenue Q
Cabaret
Def Poetry Jam
Exonerated
Menopause Music
Movin' Out
Naked Boys
Our Lady 121 St.

Rent
Take Me Out
Urban Cowboy

Notable Openings
Dream a Little
Enchanted April
Golda's Balcony
Gypsy
Joe Egg
Last Sunday
Life (x) 3
Look of Love
Nine
Play I Wrote
Salome
Talking Heads
Zanna, Don't!

Revivals
Cabaret
Chicago
42nd Street
Gypsy
Joe Egg
Man of La Mancha
Nine

Significant Playwrights
Golda's Balcony, *William Gibson*
Joe Egg, *Peter Nichols*
Life (x) 3, *Yazmina Reza*
Our Lady 121 St., *Stephen Adly Guirgis*
Salome, *Oscar Wilde*
Take Me Out, *Richard Greenberg*

Star Vehicles
Cabaret
Enchanted April
Golda's Balcony
Gypsy
Hairspray
Man of La Mancha
Nine
Play I Wrote
Say G'dnight Gracie
Talking Heads
Tea at Five

Thought-Provoking
Cabaret
Chicago
Def Poetry Jam
Exonerated
Joe Egg
Life (x) 3
Our Lady 121 St.
Rent
Talking Heads
Women of Lockerbie

Tony Award Winners
(Best Play or Musical)
Les Mis
Lion King
Phantom of Opera
Producers
Rent
Thoroughly MM

Restaurants

Key to Ratings/Symbols

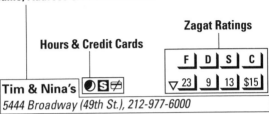

Name, Address & Phone Number

Zagat Ratings

Hours & Credit Cards

F	D	S	C
▽ 23	9	13	$15

Tim & Nina's ◑ 🅂 ⊘

5444 Broadway (49th St.), 212-977-6000

◪ Open 24/7, this "literal dive" is located in the IND station under Columbus Circle; as NY's first subway "kebab and soul pizza" stand, it offers "preposterous" pies with toppings of BBQ sauce and shish kebab to harried strap-hangers "for little dough"; but for the "cost of your MetroCard" and the "need to shout your order" when the A train comes in, this would be "some trip."

Review, with surveyors' comments in quotes

Before reviews a symbol indicates whether responses were uniform ■ or mixed ◪.

Hours: ◑ serves after 11 PM
🅂 open on Sunday

Credit Cards: ⊘ no credit cards accepted

Ratings: Food, Decor and Service are rated on a scale of **0** to **30**. The Cost (C) column reflects our surveyors' estimate of the price of dinner including one drink and tip.

F Food	D Decor	S Service	C Cost
23	9	13	$15

0–9 poor to fair	**20–25** very good to excellent
10–15 fair to good	**26–30** extraordinary to perfection
16–19 good to very good	▽ low response/less reliable

For places listed without ratings or a numerical cost estimate, such as an important newcomer or a popular write-in, the price range is indicated by the following symbols.

I	$15 and below	**E**	$31 to $50
M	$16 to $30	**VE**	$51 or more

Top Rated Restaurants

Excluding places with low votes.

Top Theater District

Food

28 Le Bernardin
    Sugiyama
26 La Côte Basque
    La Caravelle
    Aquavit

Decor

26 FireBird
    Le Bernardin
    Aquavit
    La Côte Basque
25 La Caravelle

Service

27 Le Bernardin
26 La Caravelle
25 La Côte Basque
    Aquavit
23 Il Tinello

Most Popular

1. Le Bernardin
2. Aquavit
3. Palm West
4. La Côte Basque
5. Haru

Top Union Square

Food

27 Gramercy Tavern
    Veritas
    Union Sq. Cafe
26 Craft
24 Tocqueville

Decor

25 Gramercy Tavern
    Craft
    AZ
23 Tamarind
    Union Sq. Cafe

Service

27 Gramercy Tavern
26 Union Sq. Cafe
    Veritas
24 Craft
23 Tocqueville

Most Popular

1. Gramercy Tavern
2. Union Sq. Cafe
3. Blue Water Grill
4. Craft
5. Mesa Grill

Top Village

Food

27 Gotham B&G
    Il Mulino
    Babbo
    Tomoe Sushi
26 Jewel Bako

Decor

27 One if by Land, TIBS
25 Gotham B&G
    Jewel Bako
23 Babbo
    Strip House

Service

25 Gotham B&G
    Tasting Room
    One if by Land
24 Il Mulino
    Babbo

Most Popular

1. Gotham B&G
2. Babbo
3. Il Mulino
4. Yama
5. One if by Land

Top by Special Feature

Child-Friendly
23 Shaffer City
Campagna
22 City Bakery
Chur. Plataforma
21 John's Pizzeria

Expense Account
28 Le Bernardin
Sugiyama
27 Gramercy Tavern
Gotham B&G
Il Mulino

"In" Places
27 Gramercy Tavern
Veritas
Babbo
26 Craft
Tasting Room

Late-Dining
24 Joe's Pizza
23 Corner Bistro
Blue Water Grill
22 SushiSamba
Haru

Outdoor
25 Lupa
Milos
Hasaki
Blue Hill
Sushi Zen

Prix Fixe
28 Le Bernardin
27 Gramercy Tavern
Veritas
26 La Côte Basque
La Caravelle

Quick Bites
25 Mexicana Mama
24 Amy's Bread
23 'ino
22 Island Burgers
City Bakery

Quiet Conversation
27 Gramercy Tavern
Veritas
Union Sq. Cafe
25 Blue Hill
One if by Land

Romantic
25 Blue Hill
One if by Land
23 Chez Michallet
AZ
ViceVersa

Sunday
27 Gramercy Tavern
Gotham B&G
Veritas
Babbo
Union Sq. Cafe

subscribe to zagat.com

Pre-Theater Prix Fixes

Aquavit	32.00	Lanza	18.50
AZ	57.00	Le Beaujolais	24.00
Beacon	35.00	Le Bernardin	84.00
Becco	21.95	Le Rivage	25.75
Bryant Park	25.00	Martini's	20.02
Cascina (9th Ave.)	24.50	Michael's	38.00
Charlotte	39.50	Milos	45.00
Chez Michallet	22.95	Molyvos	34.50
Chur. Plataforma	39.95	One if by Land	63.00
Cité	49.00	Osteria del Circo	32.00
Cité Grill	49.00	Pergola/Artistes	from 20.00
Cucina di Pesce	10.95	Pierre au Tunnel	34.00
db Bistro Moderne	39.00	Pigalle	24.95
Del Frisco's	34.95	René Pujol	42.00
FireBird	38.00	Russian Samovar	25.00
44	44.00	Sardi's	43.50
Gramercy Tavern	68.00	Shaan	21.95
Hourglass Tavern	15.75	Strip House	49.00
Ilo	39.00	Sushiden	35.00
Kitchen 22	25.00	Thalia	30.03
La Belle Epoque	25.00	Trattorio Dopo	22.50
La Caravelle	72.00	'21' Club	37.00
La Côte Basque	70.00	Veritas	68.00
La Metairie	25.00	ViceVersa	30.03

Amy's Bread 🆂 ⌀　　　　24 | 11 | 15 | $12
672 Ninth Ave. (bet. 46th & 47th Sts.), 212-977-2670
■ As "addictive" as "manna", the "untypical" varieties of "knockout breads" for "low dough" make this bakery/cafe a major "destination"; the "delights" extend to sandwiches and "wicked" baked goods, though "postage-stamp" seating makes most grab their "goodies to go."

Angelo & Maxie's 🆂　　　　20 | 18 | 18 | $49
233 Park Ave. S. (19th St.), 212-220-9200
1285 Sixth Ave. (52nd St.), 212-459-1222
☑ Relive the "'80s again" at this "kicking" steakhouse duo where "corporate types" practice "cigar chomping" and cut their "red-meat" teeth on "macho" slabs of beef; expect a "hearty meal" at a "fair price", but given the smoke and noise, pack a "gas mask" and a pair of "earplugs."

Angelo's Pizzeria 🆂　　　　21 | 11 | 14 | $22
117 W. 57th St. (bet. 6th & 7th Aves.), 212-333-4333
☑ For those "midweek energy slumps", this Midtown pizza parlor turns out "impressive" "coal-fired" pies that "rival John's" with their "superthin, crispy crusts" and "fresh toppings"; so more's the pity that service is so "slow."

Angus McIndoe ❶🆂　　　▽ 18 | 17 | 18 | $41
258 W. 44th St. (bet. B'way & 8th Ave.), 212-221-9222
☑ "After years at Joe Allen", its "gracious" maitre d' has opened this eponymous tri-level Theater District American, a "showbizzy" "actors hangout" where the "stuff of gossip columns" plays out nightly; its "tasty but not wonderful" food doesn't distract from all the "stargazing."

Anju　　　　　　　　　– | – | – | M
(fka Remedy)
36 E. 20th St. (bet. B'way & Park Ave. S.), 212-674-1111
Not so much a cure as an alternative to the Flatiron District's dining favorites, this swank new Korean-American–cum–lounge offers BBQ prepared at the table, plus a full menu.

Annisa 🆂　　　　　　25 | 21 | 23 | $59
13 Barrow St. (bet. 7th Ave. S. & W. 4th St.),
212-741-6699
■ "Dynamite" New American cooking from "food goddess" Anita Lo is the raison d'être of this "soothing" West Village "gem"; it's a bit "precious" portion-wise, but nevertheless so "welcoming" and "tranquil" that few mind embarking on an "expense-account binge" here.

Aquavit 🆂　　　　　　26 | 26 | 25 | $64
13 W. 54th St. (bet. 5th & 6th Aves.), 212-307-7311
■ A "chic" "spa" for the "palate and eyes", chef Marcus Samuelsson's Scandinavian Midtowner turns out "avant-garde" feats of "incredible herring-do" abetted by "flawless service" and a "sleek", "head-turning" atrium setting complete with a "dramatic waterfall" and birch trees;

salmon "sticker-shock" survivors suggest a calming "infusion" of the eponymous "water of life" – or a spell in the more af-fjordable "upstairs cafe."

Arezzo
22 | 15 | 20 | $55

46 W. 22nd St. (bet. 5th & 6th Aves.), 212-206-0555
☑ Already "quite a scene", this Flatiron Italian yearling "fills a niche" as a "small but accommodating" source of "delicious seasonal" cooking paired with "solicitous" service; on the downside are "astronomical prices" that seem out of place in such a "no-frills", "minimalist" setting.

A Salt & Battery S
– | – | – | I

112 Greenwich Ave. (bet. 12th & 13th Sts.), 212-691-2713
80 Second Ave. (bet. 4th & 5th Sts.), 212-254-6610
Anglophiles are aglow over the latest additions to NY's expanding British empire: an authentic fish 'n' chips pair (a West Village take-out and an East Village sit-down novice) where deep-fried fillets come wrapped in newspaper.

AZ S
23 | 25 | 22 | $60

21 W. 17th St. (bet. 5th & 6th Aves.), 212-691-8888
■ "Amazin' Asian" accents make the "fabulous flavor" combos taste "az good az" they look at chef Patricia Yeo's "slick-as-they-come" Flatiron New American replete with a "swanky lounge" downstairs and "magic elevator" ride to the "serene" upstairs dining room under a "retractable glass roof"; though a few feel it's "overpriced", devotees are "dazzled" "from A to Z."

Babbo ●S
27 | 23 | 24 | $66

110 Waverly Pl. (bet. MacDougal St. & 6th Ave.), 212-777-0303
■ Ever "pushing the culinary envelope", this "magnifico" Village "showstopper" from (Molto Mario) Batali and (just plain Joe) Bastianich showcases "robust", "adventurous" Italian cooking with "bold" techniques that make for "heaven on a plate"; the "bella" bi-level townhouse setting and "warm, efficient" staff ("despite the mobs") set the "simply luxe" tone, and though getting a table is akin to winning the "Powerball lottery", "all those limos outside can't be wrong" – it's as good as a trip to Rome.

Barbetta ●
20 | 23 | 20 | $55

321 W. 46th St. (bet. 8th & 9th Aves.), 212-246-9171
■ With a "romantic" interior and a "corner-of-paradise" courtyard, this Restaurant Row Northern Italian landmark (circa 1906) maintains a "grand" style that extends to its first-rate food and "genteel", black-tie service; though sometimes slighted as a "faded rose", it really blooms "after the pre-theater rush is over."

Bay Leaf S
21 | 18 | 18 | $36

49 W. 56th St. (bet. 5th & 6th Aves.), 212-957-1818
■ "Pleasant" and "prettier than most", this Midtown siren of "fine Indian dining" is notable for a "best-buy lunch buffet"

that's easy on the wallet but tough on the waistline; though the dinner prices "aren't cheap", at least the "varied" menu is always a "treat for the taste buds."

Beacon
22 | 21 | 20 | $54

25 W. 56th St. (bet. 5th & 6th Aves.), 212-332-0500

■ A "shining light" in Midtown, this New American features "honest", "wood-fired cooking" from "talented" chef Waldy Malouf that "totally works" as a "palate pleaser" (just "don't tell the red-meat police"); the "handsome" "multi-level" setup featuring a "view of the kitchen" is so "relaxed" and "civilized", few are daunted by the prices.

Becco ⬤S
20 | 17 | 19 | $39

355 W. 46th St. (bet. 8th & 9th Aves.), 212-397-7597

■ "Sometimes better than the show" (and always cheaper), the "amazing" $21.95 "all-you-can-eat pasta" special at this "homey" Theater District Northern Italian is a "big-appetite" magnet; since it's a perennial "top choice", either "book in advance" or go late.

Ben Benson's S
23 | 17 | 20 | $59

123 W. 52nd St. (bet. 6th & 7th Aves.), 212-581-8888

■ Supplying enough "old-school meat" to sate your "inner caveman", this "raucous" Midtown chophouse specializes in "two-cows-per-serving" porterhouses and drinks "you could take a bath in" (along with "clipped" service and "relentlessly" macho surroundings); if it doesn't always live up to its advertising, at least it's "predictable" "in a good way" – just be man enough for the tabs.

Beppe
22 | 21 | 20 | $53

45 E. 22nd St. (bet. B'way & Park Ave. S.), 212-982-8422

■ As "inviting" as a "rustic" holiday, this Flatiron Tuscan "stands out" with chef Cesare Casella's "creative" cooking in an "understated" "farmhouse" setting staffed by "cheery professionals"; if some say it's "overpriced", most agree its "flair" alone is "worth every" centesimo.

Blue Fin ⬤S
21 | 22 | 18 | $51

W Hotel Times Sq., 1567 Broadway (47th St.), 212-918-1400

■ "Finally, quality and sophistication" sail into Times Square aboard Steve Hanson's new "eye-popping" double-decker "tour de force" in the W Hotel, where a "snazzy clientele" nibbles "delish" seafood delicacies in a "swanky" setting (complete with a "window-walled" "fishbowl" bar up front); the food is almost an "added bonus" to the "slick" scenery, though sinkers include "foghorn"-loud acoustics and "platinum prices."

Blue Hill S
25 | 22 | 23 | $58

75 Washington Pl. (bet. 6th Ave. & Washington Sq. W.), 212-539-1776

■ They're "on top of their game" at this "refined" New American "piece of heaven" in a "stylish" Greenwich

Village brownstone where diners find their thrill with chefs Daniel Barber and Michael Anthony's "superb", "spot-on cuisine" delivered with "panache" by a "gracious staff"; it's a "distinctive treat" for "grown-ups" that's "well worth" the price, though the "pretty" room may be "a little crowded" with "even prettier people."

Blue Water Grill ●S   23 | 22 | 20 | $47
31 Union Sq. W. (16th St.), 212-675-9500
■ Union Square harbors this "perpetual favorite" from Steve Hanson, an "on-target" specialist in "scrumptious seafood" served on two floors in a "spacious" "restored bank" that boasts a "wraparound" "outdoor balcony" and "cool jazz downstairs"; with a "sparkling" raw bar, "excellent" brunch and "accommodating staff", it's always "abuzz" with "pretty people" seeking "action."

Bolo S   22 | 20 | 20 | $52
23 E. 22nd St. (bet. B'way & Park Ave. S.), 212-228-2200
■ "Bold flavors" and a "colorful, upbeat space" deliver a "real kick" at Bobby Flay's Flatiron Spaniard where the "imaginative" contemporary fare "served with flair" will "wake the senses" (ditto the price tags); after "all the brouhaha", a few "expect moor" from "Mr. Food Network", but most are bowled over by this "impressive" "knockout."

Bond Street ●S   25 | 22 | 18 | $54
6 Bond St. (bet. B'way & Lafayette St.), 212-777-2500
■ "If you still have an expense account", check out this NoHo "premium Japanese" where "exquisite sushi" comes in slices "minimal" enough for the appetites of the "runway set's slimmest waifs"; in its "super-trendy" downstairs lounge, the clientele is as "delectable" and "eye-opening" as the food, even if the "attitude galore" is a drag.

Bryant Park Grill/Cafe S   16 | 21 | 16 | $41
behind NY Public Library, 25 W. 40th St. (bet. 5th & 6th Aves.), 212-840-6500
◪ "Gorgeous" Bryant Park sets the scene at these "lively" Americans where the simple alfresco Cafe boasts an "unbeatable" "urban landscape" "backdrop" and the far classier window-wrapped Grill overlooks the "park at its doorstep"; after work, they're "madhouse" meat markets for "young attractives" who don't mind the "fair" food and "runway-kids" service.

B. Smith's Restaurant Row S   18 | 19 | 17 | $43
320 W. 46th St. (bet. 8th & 9th Aves.), 212-315-1100
■ TV's "Barbara Smith herself" is often on hand at this "cordial" Restaurant Row Eclectic with enough soulful "twists" to make it a "hit" for pre-theater supping with "style"; when critics call it a "tad disappointing", it's not clear whether they're talking about the restaurant or the fact that its owner is happily married.

Cafe Un Deux Trois ●S   15 | 14 | 15 | $39
123 W. 44th St. (bet. B'way & 6th Ave.), 212-354-4148
◪ "Fun", "fast and furious", this "quintessential pre-theater" French bistro off Times Square whips out "dependable", if uninspired, vittles (with a side of "crayons") in a "big, brash" room verging on "bedlam"; though it "always gets you to the show on time", critics counter that it's "tired", "touristy" and "tight" – as in crowded.

Campagna ●S   23 | 19 | 20 | $52
24 E. 21st St. (bet. B'way & Park Ave. S.), 212-460-0900
■ A "standout in a neighborhood full of them", this most "memorable" Flatiron Tuscan provides "mouthwateringly delicious" food from chef Mark Strausman in "subdued, elegant" digs enlivened by the perk of "celebrity sightings"; though prices are "fairly steep" and you may "feel a little squeezed", it remains consistently "popular."

Carnegie Deli ●S⌦   20 | 8 | 12 | $24
854 Seventh Ave. (55th St.), 212-757-2245
■ A series of "skyscraper-size sandwiches" that "would make Dagwood proud" are the bait at this "quintessential" deli in the West 50s, where NYC "locals and tourists alike" squeeze into "communal tables" and endure the "appropriately crusty service" for a taste of "overstuffed" bliss; it's "legendary for a reason" and definitely "worth the occasional angioplasty."

Cascina ●   ▽ 19 | 17 | 16 | $38
647 Ninth Ave. (bet. 45th & 46th Sts.), 212-245-4422
281 Bleecker St. (Jones St.), 212-633-2941 S
■ "Tasty brick-oven pizza" and "wines supplied from its own vineyard" explain the popularity of this "unassuming" Hell's Kitchen "pre-theater gem"; though "service needs help", the "roomy", "rustic farmhouse" setting is fine as is; N.B. the Village spin-off is new and unrated.

Charlotte S   17 | 19 | 19 | $49
Millennium Broadway Hotel, 145 W. 44th St. (bet. B'way & 6th Ave.), 212-789-7508
■ "Times Square's queen of serene", this hotel New American offers "tasty" vittles in a "sedate" setting with "well-spaced tables" that actually allow for "civilized conversation"; though pricing is "tailored to expense accounts", most find that the "bargain pre-theater prix fixe" is a fine fit.

Chez Michallet S   23 | 20 | 23 | $48
90 Bedford St. (Grove St.), 212-242-8309
■ Proving that "good things come in small packages", this "tiny" but oh-so-French–feeling West Village bistro is "big on taste" and service; if pricey for the neighborhood, it's quite reasonable for the "simply breathtaking" dining experience one receives here.

Chicama S
22 | 21 | 19 | $48

ABC Carpet & Home, 35 E. 18th St. (bet. B'way & Park Ave. S.), 212-505-2233

■ "Seviche rules" at this Union Square South American where the "exciting", "well-executed" menu competes with "exotic cocktails" and a "noisy", "lively" scene; the "tab adds up quickly", but overall this "definite date place" is "fresh and original."

China Grill S
22 | 21 | 18 | $50

CBS Bldg., 60 W. 53rd St. (bet. 5th & 6th Aves.), 212-333-7788

◪ The "'80s are still alive" at this "frenetic" Midtowner where "designer" Asian-Eclectic fare is served in a stylish, "high-ceilinged" setting; though proponents insist it "only gets better with age", realists suggest you "take someone you have nothing to say to" given a noise level "louder than a Metallica concert."

Churrascaria Plataforma ◑ S
22 | 18 | 20 | $50

Belvedere Hotel, 316 W. 49th St. (bet. 8th & 9th Aves.), 212-245-0505

■ "Even Henry VIII would be stuffed" after visiting this Theater District Brazilian "gorge-teria" featuring an "endless parade" of "cooked-to-perfection" skewered meats; so "go hungry", but "don't pig out" at the salad bar or you won't make it through the rest of the "orgy."

Cité ◑ S
21 | 19 | 21 | $56

120 W. 51st St. (bet. 6th & 7th Aves.), 212-956-7100

■ If you can hold your liquor, the "all-you-can-drink wine dinner" at this "sophisticated" Midtown chophouse has got to be "the best bargain in town"; if à la carte, think "expense account", but even then most agree the "fine food", elegant deco digs and "consistently excellent service" are "worth every penny."

Cité Grill ◑ S
19 | 17 | 19 | $45

120 W. 51st St. (bet. 6th & 7th Aves.), 212-956-7262

■ "More relaxed" and "a little cheaper" than its "big brother" next door, this "reliable" Midtown steakhouse is a "sure bet for business lunches" or a "quick dinner"; the "bar's pickup scene" is "worth the price of admission alone."

City Bakery S
22 | 14 | 14 | $18

3 W. 18th St. (bet. 5th & 6th Aves.), 212-366-1414

◪ "Pastry genius" Maury Rubin's "tarts make hearts beat faster" and co-exist with "market fresh" soups, salads and sandwiches at this "sprawling" Flatiron bakery/cafe; "sugar junkies" find everything too "irresistible" to care about little details like decor and service.

Corner Bistro ◑ S ⬦
23 | 8 | 11 | $14

331 W. Fourth St. (Jane St.), 212-242-9502

◪ Carnivores "dream about the killer burgers" at this longtime Village "dump" and their reverie isn't ruffled by

the "paper plates", "barfly decor" and "grumpy waiters";
just "bring a book" in case of "unbelievable" waits.

Craft 🅂　　　　　26 | 25 | 24 | $65

43 E. 19th St. (bet. B'way & Park Ave. S.), 212-780-0880

■ "Fresh ingredients, simply prepared" are the hallmarks of
Tom Colicchio's "casually classy" Flatiron New American
offering a "culinary abacus menu" that allows you to "add or
subtract items to build the perfect meal"; with "helpful"
servers and "dramatic decor that's yin to the food's yang",
it's "absolutely out-of-this-world", and despite "forking over
some major change" for the privilege, it's worth it – there's
"more art than craft" going on here.

Crispo ◗🅂　　　　　– | – | – | M

240 W. 14th St. (bet. 7th & 8th Aves.), 212-229-1818

From ex Zeppole chef Frank Crispo comes this attractive,
brick-lined Village Italian fronting busy 14th Street; the
neighborhood already is warming up to its appealing roster
of salads, house-made pastas and other well-priced dishes,
not to mention that friendly front bar.

Cucina di Pesce ◗🅂⊅　　　　18 | 13 | 16 | $26

87 E. Fourth St. (bet. Bowery & 2nd Ave.), 212-260-6800

■ "Frugal types love the $10.95 early-bird" deal at this East
Village Italian boasting "yummy fish specials" and "no
pretenses"; if you're willing to endure the "mob scene" later
on, there's relief in its "secret garden" and skylit back room,
despite the "guilt" at "paying so little."

Da Tommaso ◗🅂　　　　　20 | 13 | 19 | $41

903 Eighth Ave. (bet. 53rd & 54th Sts.), 212-265-1890

◪ "Old-style" Theater District Italian that marries a "hearty,
basic menu" with "accommodating" service; though some
find "nothing to get excited about" – particularly the "dreary
decor" – overall it's "comfortable" and fairly priced.

db Bistro Moderne 🅂　　　　24 | 21 | 22 | $60

City Club Hotel, 55 W. 44th St. (bet. 5th & 6th Aves.), 212-391-2400

■ "Daniel Boulud goes modern" at this "stylish" Theater
District French bistro offering the same "crafty" cooking
as the rest of his empire but at "more approachable prices";
famed for its $28 foie gras–stuffed burger, it's also known as
a "power-lunch" locus for the publishing and rag trades,
with the celebs favoring its "more formal" rear dining room.

Del Frisco's ◗🅂　　　　　23 | 23 | 21 | $64

1221 Sixth Ave. (49th St.), 212-575-5129

■ The spirit of "Gordon Gekko lives" on at this enormous
Midtown chophouse imported from Dallas that overachieves
with "sizzling" steaks, "standout sides" and an "elegant",
multi-level space that corrals "power-lunchers" by day and
power–"cigar smokers" at night; the "Texas-size" tabs
make it an "expense-accounter if there ever was one";
P.S. the private rooms are great for corporate parties.

District S   21 | 21 | 20 | $51
Muse Hotel, 130 W. 46th St. (bet. 6th & 7th Aves.), 212-485-2999
■ "Not your normal Theater District joint", this "hidden treat
in a cute boutique hotel" offers a "limited but intriguing"
menu of New American standards orchestrated by chef
Sam DeMarco; despite the "'80s prices", overall this "boffo"
act is "worthy of applause."

Esca ◑S   24 | 19 | 20 | $58
402 W. 43rd St. (9th Ave.), 212-564-7272
■ Chef David Pasternack continues to produce "exquisite"
seafood and "sublime pastas" at this attractive Theater
District Italian, a Batali/Bastianich project that also wins
fans with outdoor dining; though "lunch is a bargain", "it
helps to have an expense account" at dinner.

FireBird S   21 | 26 | 22 | $58
365 W. 46th St. (bet. 8th & 9th Aves.), 212-586-0244
■ "Like a Tolstoy novel – without the dreary relatives" – this
"imperial jewel box" set in a Restaurant Row townhouse
is like "dining with the tsar" with its "different"-but-
"delicious" Russian fare, "exotic" vodka infusions, "divine"
duplex setup and "regal" service; in short, "you won't be
disappointed" "visually or gastronomically"; if you miss
the Russian Tea Room, this place is for you.

Fives S   – | – | – | E
(fka Adrienne)
Peninsula Hotel, 700 Fifth Ave. (55th St.), 212-903-3918
After years of relative anonymity, this lovely restaurant in
the Peninsula Hotel has expanded its New American
menu and turned its adjacent cafe into an inviting wine bar;
whether these changes will succeed in overcoming its
mezzanine location is anyone's guess.

Fleur de Sel S   23 | 18 | 21 | $62
5 E. 20th St. (bet. B'way & 5th Ave.), 212-460-9100
■ At this "elegant Left Bank transplant" "hidden in the
Flatiron", the "inspired", "genuinely gourmet" Gallic fare and
"thoughtful, unobtrusive service" are "fit for royalty"; even
though the spare, "minimalist decor" and "Fifth Avenue
prices" turn off some, most surveyors agree that this "flower
is in full bloom."

Fontana di Trevi S   ▽ 19 | 16 | 21 | $40
151 W. 57th St. (bet. 6th & 7th Aves.), 212-247-5683
■ "You don't last [45 years] without delivering the goods",
and this "civilized" Northern Italian near Carnegie Hall has
regulars "coming back again and again" for its good "old-
fashioned" cooking and "accommodating service."

44 S   – | – | – | VE
Royalton Hotel, 44 W. 44th St. (bet. 5th & 6th Aves.), 212-944-8844
Claude Troisgros' reworking of the New American menu
has given this trendy Midtown restaurant a big lift, drawing

pub biz types at lunch and hepcats at supper; sure, it's pricey, but it pays off with a first-class meal in stylish digs.

44 & X Hell's Kitchen ●⑤   22 | 19 | 19 | $42 |
622 10th Ave. (44th St.), 212-977-1170
■ "Mac 'n' cheese meets nouvelle" at this New American "surprise" in the "way out" West 40s, where "homespun" "designer comfort food" and "Manhattan-slick" digs come with a "view of the Hess gas station"; despite the "high noise level", it's a "welcome addition" to Hell's Kitchen.

Gallagher's Steak House ●⑤   20 | 15 | 17 | $55 |
228 W. 52nd St. (bet. B'way & 8th Ave.), 212-245-5336
☒ This "show-must-go-on" chop shop has been a "great character in the heart of the Theatre District" since 1927, proudly displaying its wares in a "windowed meat locker"; but those who steer clear call it "nostalgia best forgotten" due to prices that "fillet your wallet" and service "not as generous as the steaks."

Giorgio's of Gramercy ⑤   22 | 19 | 20 | $40 |
27 E. 21st St. (bet. B'way & Park Ave. S.), 212-477-0007
■ "It keeps getting better" at this up-and-coming Flatiron New American "sleeper" serving "inventive, tasty" fare that "won't burn a hole in your wallet"; since you can "talk and be heard", it's garnering a rep as a "perfect date place."

Gonzo ●⑤   – | – | – | M |
140 W. 13th St. (bet. 6th & 7th Aves.), 212-645-4606
Chef Vincent Scotto (ex Scopa) heads south with his trademark tasty pizzas, pastas and steaks to this friendly, midpriced West Village Italian; first-timers may be surprised by its scale, with a soaring ceiling and plenty of space that far exceeds the area's typical pocket-size places.

Gotham Bar & Grill ⑤   27 | 25 | 25 | $63 |
12 E. 12th St. (bet. 5th Ave. & University Pl.), 212-620-4020
■ This "elegant" Village New American is where "genius at work" Alfred Portale "still reigns", concocting "towering", "skyscraper"-like presentations that taste as good as they look; "faultless service" and "airy" environs shore up this annual winner's "staying power", as does the "deal-of-a-lifetime" $25.00 prix fixe lunch.

Gramercy Tavern ⑤   27 | 25 | 27 | $68 |
42 E. 20th St. (bet. B'way & Park Ave. S.), 212-477-0777
■ "As good as everyone says it is", Danny Meyer's Flatiron "triumph" has become an established NY favorite thanks to chef Tom Colicchio's "pure and passionate" New American creations, "exquisite" desserts, service that's "perfection personified" and handsome, neo-colonial decor; loyalties are divided between the "less pricey" "drop-in" bar area and the "more formal back rooms", but wherever you choose to sit, this is a "priceless experience"; P.S. try not to "hug the waiter."

Grand Sichuan 🅂   23 | 8 | 14 | $23
745 Ninth Ave. (bet. 50th & 51st Sts.), 212-582-2288
▣ For "something different from the same old Chinese", this eatery offers "endless selections" of "hot and spicy treats" at "budget prices"; maybe the service and setting aren't as "Mao-velous" as the chow, but the "book-length menu" provides plenty of distraction.

Haru ◑🅂   22 | 17 | 16 | $37
205 W. 43rd St. (bet. B'way & 8th Ave.), 212-398-9810
■ Rolling out "Moby Dick–size" portions of "sublime" sushi, this "hip" Japanese also serves other "excellent entrees" at prices that "may tip (but won't break) the scales"; it's "mandatory dining" for most, though some say "sayonara" to the "out-the-door lines."

Hasaki ◑🅂   25 | 14 | 18 | $37
210 E. Ninth St. (bet. 2nd & 3rd Aves.), 212-473-3327
■ "Skip lunch and go early" to this way-too-"popular" Alphabet City Japanese that's "legendary" for its "silky-fresh sushi", "reasonable" price tags and "no-reservations policy" – all of which naturally add up to "big waits"; the only other disappointment comes "when the meal ends."

Hell's Kitchen 🅂   24 | 18 | 19 | $38
679 Ninth Ave. (bet. 46th & 47th Sts.), 212-977-1588
■ Chef Jorje Pareja's "clever" Nouveau Mexican cooking keeps this modest Theater District cantina (aka the "poor man's Mesa Grill") always "packed"; his myriad fans insist it's worth enduring the "long waits" and "close quarters" for a taste of the "delicioso" eats.

Hourglass Tavern ◑🅂   14 | 13 | 16 | $27
373 W. 46th St. (bet. 8th & 9th Aves.), 212-265-2060
▣ "Funky and cheap", this "reliable" Restaurant Row American has a "gimmick" – you'll be "in and out in less than 60 minutes" – guaranteeing you'll make your curtain; trade-offs are "spotty" grub, "claustrophobic", pie-slice digs and service that's fast but not always friendly.

Il Mulino ◑   27 | 18 | 24 | $74
86 W. Third St. (bet. Sullivan & Thompson Sts.), 212-673-3783
■ "If you need a challenge", just "try getting reservations" at this mind-bogglingly popular Villager; it could pack them in with its "aromas alone" – though the "perfectly prepared" food and "impeccable" black-tie service aren't a handicap either; so "beg, lie, cheat or sell your soul to the devil" and "keep hitting redial" – "it's worth it" for the "best car payment" you'll ever eat; P.S. lunch is easier.

Ilo 🅂   24 | 22 | 22 | $74
Bryant Park Hotel, 40 W. 40th St. (bet. 5th & 6th Aves.), 212-642-2255
■ Ever since chef Rick Laakkonen (ex River Cafe) opened this "vibrant" New American on Bryant Park, "serious

foodies" have been flocking here; they report feeling "pure joy" as a result of the "clear, subtle flavors", "sparkling service", "pristine surroundings" and "high-fashion", "glitterati" crowd; only the prices and "relentless noise from the nearby bar" provoke any discord.

Il Tinello   23 | 19 | 23 | $58
16 W. 56th St. (bet. 5th & 6th Aves.), 212-245-4388
■ "Attention to detail" keeps this Midtown Northern Italian popular with an "older business crowd" that shows up for its "excellent food" and "solicitous service"; though a bit too "traditional" (verging on "stodgy") for modernists, overall it's reliably "nice and easygoing."

'ino ●◗⬛⊄   23 | 15 | 18 | $21
21 Bedford St. (bet. Downing St. & 6th Ave.),
212-989-5769
■ For "sandwich perfection", it's hard to beat this West Village panini purveyor also known for a swell "selection of wines by the glass"; the "bite-size food" comes in a bite-size space, but its large following seems more than willing to wait for a "coveted table."

Island Burgers & Shakes ⬛⊄   22 | 7 | 14 | $15
766 Ninth Ave. (bet. 51st & 52nd Sts.), 212-307-7934
☑ "Killer shakes" and "more varieties of burgers than you ever thought possible" fill the menu of this Hell's Kitchen "dive"; many don't understand why they "don't have fries" and suggest takeout, as the "decor is better unexperienced."

Iso ◗   24 | 14 | 17 | $38
175 Second Ave. (11th St.), 212-777-0361
■ Schools of "discerning sushi seekers" surface at this "deservedly popular", "reasonably priced" East Village Japanese establishment; "long lines are the norm" because "they don't take reservations."

Jewel Bako   26 | 25 | 23 | $61
239 E. Fifth St. (bet. 2nd & 3rd Aves.), 212-979-1012
■ "Exquisite attention to detail" is the hallmark of this "adventurous" East Village Japanese that "takes sushi so seriously" that you "can't go wrong with the freshness and quality"; kudos abound for its "charming owners" and ultra-"calming" ambiance ("like walking into another dimension"), and though portions are "small", prices "sky high" and reservations "difficult", it's worth the effort for one of the "best splurges" in town.

Jezebel ⬛   19 | 24 | 18 | $48
630 Ninth Ave. (45th St.), 212-582-1045
☑ "You can practically smell the bougainvillea" at this Theater District standby known for its "*Gone With the Wind*" "bordello" decor, "porch swings and all"; while most find the Southern cooking "lick-your-fingers" good, critics insist it's "more fun-worthy than food-worthy."

Joe Allen ◗🅂　　　16 | 15 | 17 | $38

326 W. 46th St. (bet. 8th & 9th Aves.), 212-581-6464

◪ "Bring cousin Edna from Moline and a flash camera" to this "Theater District tradition" that's popular with show folk, "wanna-bes and onlookers"; despite "nothing-special" decor and nearly "nonexistent service", the American chow is "decent" and the mood "lively", especially when a celeb sits down at the next table.

Joe's Pizza 🅂　　　24 | 4 | 14 | $9

233 Bleecker St. (Carmine St.), 212-366-1182 ◗
7 Carmine St. (bet. Bleecker St. & 6th Ave.), 212-255-3946

◪ This "no-frills" Village pizza parlor pair "sets the standard" with "great crust, great cheese and great sauce", although "no decor" and "no service" are also part of the package; at least they're "open late" and the "wild street life" outside is something to behold.

John's Pizzeria ◗🅂　　　21 | 12 | 14 | $20

278 Bleecker St. (bet. 6th Ave. & 7th Ave. S.), 212-243-1680 ⊄
260 W. 44th St. (bet. B'way & 8th Ave.), 212-391-7560

■ "Heavenly thin-crust" pizzas lure legions to endure "mile-long lines" and an occasional side of "attitude" at this original Village "brick-oven epicenter" (or its more modern Uptown location); they don't serve slices, but "you'll want to eat the whole pie anyway."

JUdson Grill　　　22 | 21 | 20 | $55

152 W. 52nd St. (bet. 6th & 7th Aves.), 212-582-5252

■ A "savvy spot for power-lunching", this "spacious, gracious" Midtowner is also a "beautiful showcase" for chef Bill Telepan's "imaginative" New American food, delivered by a "hard-working" staff; brace yourself for a roaring "Hamptons-like bar scene" after work.

Kitchen 22　　　– | – | – | M

(fka Alva)
36 E. 22nd St. (bet. B'way & Park Ave. S.), 212-228-4399

Charlie Palmer has joined the comfort-food revolution at this easygoing new Flatiron American built around a $25 three-course prix fixe menu that changes frequently; even the martinis are comfortingly priced at $7.50 a pop.

Kyma ◗🅂　　　20 | 16 | 18 | $38

300 W. 46th St. (8th Ave.), 212-957-8830

■ Flaunting "authentic", "home-cooked" flavors, this "convenient" Theater District Greek is waiting to be discovered for its "tasty basics", "sweet service" and "reasonable prices"; it's an "accommodating" option for the Broadway-bound.

La Belle Epoque ◗🅂　　　▽ 14 | 22 | 14 | $41

827 Broadway (bet. 12th & 13th Sts.), 212-254-6436

◪ "It's not the food, but the tango" nights and "festive" jazz brunch that keep this Village French-Creole popular;

though its "bordello-chic" is "beautiful", "inattentive" service and "mediocre" food lead many to conclude "not up to par."

La Caravelle
26 │ 25 │ 26 │ $80

33 W. 55th St. (bet. 5th & 6th Aves.), 212-586-4252
■ Proving that "true civilization does exist in NY", André and Rita Jammet's fortysomething Midtown French "favorite" maintains its "old-world perfection" via chef Troy Dupuy's "top-notch" creations, a warmly "posh" setting and a staff that "knows what you want before you do"; despite "jet set" dinner prices (prix fixe only, $72), it's a $38 bargain for lunch; devotees insist "there is a heaven – and you don't have to die to get there."

La Côte Basque S
26 │ 26 │ 25 │ $75

60 W. 55th St. (bet. 5th & 6th Aves.), 212-688-6525
■ "Like coming home – if you live in Versailles" – this "flawless French" Midtowner has supporters sighing over Jean-Jacques Rachou's "sublime" food, the "lush" setting (decorated with paintings of the Basque seacoast) and the "formal" yet "comfortable" service; sure, it's "pricey" (prix fixe $70 dinner) but "quicker than the Concord" for that "vacation to France like it used to be"; indeed, many say this "grande dame" only "improves with age" – and the $38 prix fixe lunch costs less than taxi fare to the airport.

La Metairie S
21 │ 20 │ 20 │ $51

189 W. 10th St. (W. 4th St.), 212-989-0343
■ As if "plucked from Provence", this "charming" French West Villager supplies "wonderful meals" enhanced by a "great wine list" and "solicitous service"; though "'intimate' is a polite adjective" for the seating, overall this "civilized outpost" is "in a class all by itself."

Lanza Restaurant S
16 │ 13 │ 17 │ $30

168 First Ave. (bet. 10th & 11th Sts.), 212-674-7014
◪ "You could be on a movie set" at this circa-1904 East Village Italian where the "ghosts of dons past" and "good old-fashioned red sauce" vie for your attention; though some say the menu is "showing its age", at least pricing "won't break the bank."

La Pizza Fresca Ristorante S
22 │ 16 │ 18 │ $31

31 E. 20th St. (bet. B'way & Park Ave. S.), 212-598-0141
■ An "adorable little" Flatiron Italian trattoria turning out "customized" Neapolitan brick-oven pizzas and "excellent pastas" that taste even better when complemented by its "amazing" wines; though "service can be variable", overall things are "*molto bene*" here.

La Rivista
▽ 18 │ 15 │ 17 │ $44

313 W. 46th St. (bet. 8th & 9th Aves.), 212-245-1707
◪ "It has the location" to be a "dependable" opener to a "Broadway show", and this Restaurant Row Italian

follows through with "quite good" food and live piano music;
they even throw in "free parking" vouchers.

Lattanzi ◐ | 22 | 19 | 20 | $49 |
361 W. 46th St. (bet. 8th & 9th Aves.), 212-315-0980
■ Never mind Broadway, fans say the Lattanzi family
deserves its own "cooking show" based on the "classic
Roman-style" dishes at this "top-notch" Restaurant Row
Italian; patrons applaud the "efficient handling" pre-theater
and enjoy basking in the "warm ambiance."

Le Beaujolais ⑤ | 17 | 12 | 17 | $37 |
364 W. 46th St. (bet. 8th & 9th Aves.), 212-974-7464
◪ "Value" seekers sense "a certain charm" in this old-time
Restaurant Row French bistro, especially the "easy-on-the-
budget" "pre-theater special"; but "despite the range of
choices", some say the "tired" routine holds "no surprises."

Le Bernardin | 28 | 26 | 27 | $88 |
155 W. 51st St. (bet. 6th & 7th Aves.), 212-554-1515
■ "Hallowed ground" for gourmets, Maguy LeCoze's
Midtown French "piscatorial paradise" "spoils you" with
"incredible" feats of "culinary magic" from chef Eric
Ripert and "seamless service" in a "gorgeous" setting;
"breathless" admirers don't mind the "whale of a bill" (prix
fixe lunch $47, dinner $84), since this is dining "nonpareil."

Le Madeleine ⑤ | 20 | 18 | 19 | $42 |
403 W. 43rd St. (bet. 9th & 10th Aves.), 212-246-2993
■ "For many years" showgoers have "depended" on this
"no-pretense" Hell's Kitchen French bistro for "satisfying"
food and "friendly" service; however, those who arrive after
the "crazy" "pre-theater rush" can "really relax" and
"enjoy" the "attractive" experience.

Le Rivage ⑤ | 18 | 15 | 19 | $38 |
340 W. 46th St. (bet. 8th & 9th Aves.), 212-765-7374
◪ "Solid" if "not terribly exciting", this Restaurant Row
French "caters to the theater crowd" with a "fair-priced"
set menu and "friendly" service that "gets you out" "fast";
despite "plain" digs, it provides a "pleasant" experience.

Lupa ◐⑤ | 25 | 18 | 20 | $44 |
170 Thompson St. (bet. Bleecker & Houston Sts.), 212-982-5089
■ Tables are "hard to come by" at this "terrific" West
Village trattoria that "draws throngs" with an "exciting",
"robust" "revelation of simple Italian cooking" that's "justa
lika Roma" at its most "exciting"; the "convivial" ambiance,
"courteous staff" and "moderate prices" confirm that
owners Batali, Bastianich and Denton "can do no wrong."

Marseille ⑤ | 22 | 20 | 19 | $48 |
630 Ninth Ave. (44th St.), 212-333-2323
■ A "red-hot" hit in the Theater District, this "snazzy" new
Med brasserie performs "way above par" with an "original"

menu of "fresh, fascinating" food from "terrific chef Alex Ureña" "served with flair"; the "noisy", "hopping" crowds that fill its "Casablanca"-ish space report it's "worth the bucks" – play it again, Sam.

Martini's ●⑤ 16 | 15 | 15 | $36

810 Seventh Ave. (53rd St.), 212-767-1717
☑ "There's no doubt" the "martinis rock" at this "crowded" Theater District Cal-Italian; show-goers also applaud the "enjoyable" food and the "enclosed patio", but stirred-up critics find it no great shakes.

Maxie's ●⑤ – | – | – | M

723 Seventh Ave. (48th St.), 212-398-1118
This muraled, late-night Theater District newcomer features maxi-sandwiches, desserts, people-watching and tourists galore, plus a spacious, booth-filled upstairs room ideal for locals who want to keep a low profile.

Mesa Grill ⑤ 23 | 20 | 20 | $50

102 Fifth Ave. (bet. 15th & 16th Sts.), 212-807-7400
■ "Fame hasn't spoiled" this Flatiron "perennial" where "cocky" Food Network "honcho" Bobby Flay struts his "showman" stuff with "zesty" SW fare; the "bold flay-vors" are a perfect match for the "loud", "energetic" setting, "formidable bills" and "stunning" "cactus margaritas", but on balance, the cuisine "is the star here."

Meskerem ●⑤ 23 | 10 | 16 | $23

468 W. 47th St. (bet. 9th & 10th Aves.), 212-664-0520
124 MacDougal St. (bet. Bleecker & W. 3rd Sts.), 212-777-8111
☑ Take "someone you really like" to this Ethiopian twosome because "no silverware is used" and the "addictive", "highly spiced" stews are meant "for sharing"; despite "spotty" service and "sparse settings", its "no-skimp" portions add up to "awesome deals."

Mexicana Mama ⑤⌀ 25 | 11 | 16 | $29

525 Hudson St. (bet. Charles & W. 10th Sts.), 212-924-4119
■ Mama "knows what she's doing" at this "teeny tiny" West Village "gourmet Mexican", a "huge hit" for "fresh and inventive" "culinary masterpieces" that "blow away" your typical taco; "super-cramped quarters" lead to "interminable" waits, but the payoff is "food that packs a punch" for a gentle price.

Michael's 21 | 20 | 21 | $58

24 W. 55th St. (bet. 5th & 6th Aves.), 212-767-0555
■ "LA style" sets the mellow mood at this Midtowner where "fresh", "delightful" Californian fare, a "professional", "courteous" staff and a "pretty" room adorned with "contemporary art" attract a "who's who" of "media makers"; the "bustling breakfast" and "power lunch" scenes are renowned as prime time for "deals being done."

Milos, Estiatorio ●Ⓓ⑤ | 25 | 23 | 22 | $66 |
125 W. 55th St. (bet. 6th & 7th Aves.), 212-245-7400
■ There's "no comparison" to this "first-class" Midtown Greek where "impeccable seafood" is "grilled to perfection" and seamlessly served in a "stunning", "airy" agora; finatics find "value" via the phenomenal first courses or lunch and pre-theater prix fixes, but those who elect to select from the alluring display "on ice" should "beware" of "per-pound pricing" that requires "pockets as deep as the ocean."

Molyvos ●Ⓓ⑤ | 23 | 20 | 20 | $49 |
871 Seventh Ave. (bet. 55th & 56th Sts.), 212-582-7500
■ To fulfill those "Grecian yearnings", visit this Hellenic near City Center, a "real treat" for "stellar" food served in a "bustling", "movie-set" taverna with plenty of "hospitality" to "heighten" the effect; "boisterous" crowds and "high" tabs come with the territory, but it "doesn't get much better" "this side of Athens."

Nocello ⑤ | 21 | 17 | 19 | $39 |
257 W. 55th St. (bet. B'way & 8th Ave.), 212-713-0224
◪ A "classic Northern Italian menu" offering plenty of "experimental specials" provides "very good value" at this "cozy spot" "close to Carnegie Hall and City Center"; despite "cramped quarters", "they try to please" and usually do.

Noche ⑤ | – | – | – | E |
1604 Broadway (bet. 48th & 49th Sts.), 212-541-7070
Restaurateur David Emil (Windows on the World) and designer David Rockwell have performed some sleight of hand in creating this dramatic new Theater District New American with a Latin accent; a four-story restaurant-cum-nightclub, it pulsates with a tropical beat that's already drawing mojito-fueled crowds.

Norma's ⑤ | 25 | 20 | 21 | $33 |
Le Parker Meridien, 118 W. 57th St. (bet. 6th & 7th Aves.), 212-708-7460
■ What may be "the best breakfast in town" ("the French toast has been berry, berry good to me") is served until 3 PM at this "swanky" Midtown hotel; "it costs an arm and a leg", but it "could be called E-Normas for the size of its portions"; N.B. no dinner.

Olives ⑤ | 22 | 22 | 20 | $56 |
W Union Sq. Hotel, 201 Park Ave. S. (E. 17th St.), 212-353-8345
■ Who'd have thunk a Boston restaurant would do so well in NY? – but thanks to Todd English's efforts we now have this "marvelous" Med "indulgence" with an open kitchen and "zippy, eager servers"; though it's "hard to eat inexpensively here", you get a lot for your money, and the place is really rather "relaxing" once "you shove through the trendy bar" crowd up front.

One if by Land, TIBS ⑤　　25 ｜ 27 ｜ 25 ｜ $70
17 Barrow St. (bet. 7th Ave. S. & W. 4th St.), 212-228-0822
■ "Romance abounds" ("heard two marriage proposals during dinner") at this candlelit "historic" Village landmark that once was Aaron Burr's carriage house; adorned with a balcony, fireplace, beautiful flowers and lilting music, it almost seems superfluous to mention that prix fixes are "just about perfect" and served by staffers who "thoroughly spoil" you; but, while taking the loan to buy her ring, you'd better borrow extra to cover dinner.

Orso ◐⑤　　22 ｜ 18 ｜ 19 ｜ $49
322 W. 46th St. (bet. 8th & 9th Aves.), 212-489-7212
■ One dines beside "Broadway royalty" at this "refined" Restaurant Row Northern Italian where theatergoers and stage "stars" mingle over "delicious" pastas and pizzas from an "ever-changing menu"; call "a month in advance", and "if you're lucky" you might snare a reservation.

Osteria del Circo ⑤　　21 ｜ 23 ｜ 21 ｜ $55
120 W. 55th St. (bet. 6th & 7th Aves.), 212-265-3636
■ "Truly a circus", this colorful "high-concept" Midtown Le Cirque spin-off offers a "sublime" Tuscan menu in an "over-the-top", big top–themed setting; Sirio Maccioni's sons "definitely know what they're doing" at this "family affair" – although "having Mama Eggi around" is a big plus.

Palm West ◐⑤　　23 ｜ 16 ｜ 20 ｜ $57
250 W. 50th St. (bet. B'way & 8th Ave.), 212-333-7256
■ With "sawdust on the floor" and "caricatures of famous" customers lining the walls, this "quintessential" "NY chophouse" seems "straight out of a '20s movie" (even if the waiters "aren't as surly as they used to be"); atmosphere aside, what keeps the "manly" crowd coming back are "superb" super-size steaks and lobsters "big enough to eat you", so "bring your cardiologist" and "someone else's expense account."

Patria ⑤　　24 ｜ 22 ｜ 21 ｜ $57
250 Park Ave. S. (20th St.), 212-777-6211
■ The "top-notch, inventive" cuisine ("NY's leading South American") tangos on your taste buds at this "festive yet sophisticated" Flatironer, whose "modern" multilevel interior is nearly as "hip" as its "beautiful" crowd; those who don't want to take out a second "mortgage to pay" for dinner should try the "bargain" $20.03 prix fixe lunch.

Patsy's ⑤　　20 ｜ 14 ｜ 19 ｜ $45
236 W. 56th St. (bet B'way & 8th Ave.), 212-247-3491
☑ Nostalgists favor this circa '44 "red-sauce" Southern Italian near Carnegie Hall for its "comforting" classics and "old-NY" feel that's much the same as when it was one of "Sinatra's favorites"; critics complain of "strictly by-the-numbers" cooking and "seen-better-days" digs.

Pearl Oyster Bar　　　26 | 12 | 18 | $38
18 Cornelia St. (bet. Bleecker & W. 4th Sts.), 212-691-8211
■ It's so "tiny" you may as well be "dining in an oyster", but those willing to "wait" (and wait) for one of the 25 seats at this fantastic, modestly priced Village seafooder "don't care how cramped they are"; once you bite into Rebecca Charles' creations, you can't help but agree that you've finally found a restaurant that's actually "worthy of the hype."

Pergola des Artistes　　▽ 17 | 11 | 16 | $36
252 W. 46th St. (bet. B'way & 8th Ave.), 212-302-7500
◪ It "could use sprucing up" and the tables and chairs are so "cramped" you can "dip into your neighbor's mousse", but this Theater District French bistro earns bravos for its "good values" and "quick" staff.

Periyali　　　24 | 20 | 23 | $51
35 W. 20th St. (bet. 5th & 6th Aves.), 212-463-7890
■ Unlike the typical taverna-style Greek, this upscale Flatiron standby offers a stylish, "warm, intimate" setting as well as "unbeatably fresh", "heavenly" food that elevate it "well above the souvlaki set"; if it costs more, it offers major "swoon" factor.

Piccolo Angolo S　　24 | 12 | 20 | $33
621 Hudson St. (Jane St.), 212-229-9177
■ "Reservations are key" at this "tiny", bustling West Village Italian where there's usually a "crowd out front" anticipating "delicious", "inexpensive" "feasts of monster proportions"; the entertainment comes free from owner Renato Migliorini, who recites his encyclopedic "not-to-miss specials" list "faster than a Roger Clemens fastball."

Pierre au Tunnel S　　20 | 15 | 19 | $44
250 W. 47th St. (bet. B'way & 8th Ave.), 212-575-1220
◪ For more than 50 years this "unchanging" French bistro has been a Theater District standby, thanks to its "solid" repertoire of "reliable" food and "fast" service that gets you out to the show on time; one diner's "steady" is another's "stodgy" and a third's in need of a "face-lift."

Pigalle ◐S　　18 | 19 | 16 | $33
790 Eighth Ave. (48th St.), 212-489-2233
■ "Midnight munchies" are available "anytime you need 'em" now that there's this "lively" 24/7 Theater District French bistro; it draws a "mixed crowd" of suits, "locals and tourists" with its "decent", "bargain"-priced classics and "requisite polished-tile-floor-and-mirrors" decor — now all they need is to shine up the service *un peu.*

Pipa ◐S　　21 | 22 | 17 | $42
ABC Carpet & Home, 38 E. 19th St. (bet. B'way & Park Ave S.), 212-677-2233
■ "Dark, mysterious" and "sexy" decor, "brilliant" cocktails and "tasty" tapas attract a "young, hip" crowd "packed

like *boquerónes*" into this "lively", "alluring" Spaniard inside the Flatiron's ABC Carpet & Home store; the only quibble: all those "small servings can add up to a large bill."

Pó S　　　　　25 | 16 | 20 | $43
31 Cornelia St. (bet. Bleecker & W. 4th Sts.), 212-645-2189
■ Mario Batali is long gone, but his "trademark intensity of flavor lives on" under "excellent" chef Lee McGrath at this "enchanting" (though "cramped") West Village Italian "shoebox"; the cuisine is "superb" and the six- courses-for-$40 dinner deal may be "the best tasting menu for the buck in NY", ergo "getting a reservation is close to impossible."

Redeye Grill ◑S　　　　　20 | 18 | 18 | $49
890 Seventh Ave. (56th St.), 212-541-9000
■ Shelly Fireman's City Center–area American is a "big", "bustling", "loud" and "happy" place to savor "fresh" selections; most call it "a winner" for "business" dining, taking "out-of-towners" or just for "fun."

Remi ◑S　　　　　22 | 22 | 20 | $53
145 W. 53rd St. (bet. 6th & 7th Aves.), 212-581-4242
■ Adam Tihany's "triumph of a space" is among the many pleasures of this "elegant" Midtown "expense-accounter" where "impressive" Northern Italian fare is dished out to a roomful of "corporate regulars"; those in-the-know play name-that-CEO while waiting for the food to arrive while the on-the-move try Remi To Go next door.

René Pujol　　　　　23 | 20 | 22 | $54
321 W. 51st St. (bet. 8th & 9th Aves.), 212-246-3023
■ "Berets off" to this "refined" Theater District French and its "not fake-friendly" pro staff delivering "truly wonderful" (if "not nouvelle") cuisine amid "serene" quarters; yes, it's "pricey", but the prix fixe lunch ($23) and dinner ($42) are among "the best deals in town."

Rice 'n' Beans S　　　　　20 | 7 | 14 | $21
744 Ninth Ave. (bet. 50th & 51st Sts.), 212-265-4444
☑ Its Village branch has closed, but this "no-ambiance" Hell's Kitchen Brazilian's still kicking with its "delicious", "plentiful" fare to "fill hungry bellies" for a song; the "only drawback": the "tiny" space "gets tight."

Russian Samovar ◑S　　　　　▽ 20 | 16 | 19 | $42
256 W. 52nd St. (bet. B'way & 8th Ave.), 212-757-0168
■ "Only Aeroflot gets you closer to Moscow" than this Midtown Russian where "expats congregate" to down "authentic" standards along with "too much vodka"; weekend sing-alongs provide "a rambunctious good time."

Ruth's Chris Steak House ◑S　　　　　23 | 19 | 21 | $58
148 W. 51st St. (bet. 6th & 7th Aves.), 212-245-9600
☑ "So what if it's a chain?" muse meat eaters who gather at this handsome, dark wood–paneled Midtown outpost

of a New Orleans–based franchise to happily "clog their arteries" with "giant slabs" of "superb, buttery" beef; detractors dismiss it as a "steak-by-numbers" affair that "belongs in suburbia."

Sardi's ◐Ⓢ 17 | 20 | 18 | $49
234 W. 44th St. (bet. B'way & 8th Ave.), 212-221-8440
☑ "Soak up" some "Broadway history" at this "landmark" (since '21) Times Square Continental that's "still lovable" despite "tourist-trap" tendencies and "ho-hum" chow; "it's fun checking out" the "stars on the wall (and occasionally at the next table)", so "everyone should go at least once."

Sea Grill 24 | 23 | 22 | $57
Rockefeller Ctr., 19 W. 49th St. (bet. 5th & 6th Aves.), 212-332-7610
■ Chef "Ed Brown's way with fish is nothing short of spectacular" at this "pricey" Rock Center seafooder where the "clean, minimalist cuisine" is matched by a "picture-perfect" rinkside setting; sure, it's "a little touristy" and the "sleek" decor "borders on frigid", but there's still "no better place for a date" or "celebrating a special occasion" (especially "during the holidays").

Shaan Ⓢ 22 | 21 | 19 | $39
Rockefeller Ctr., 57 W. 48th St. (bet. 5th & 6th Aves.), 212-977-8400
■ "Now this is elegant dining" say satisfied surveyors summing up this "huge" Rockefeller Center Indian; given the "reliably high-level" cuisine, "luxurious" decor, "courtly" service and a "bargain" "lunch buffet" and $21.95 pre-theater prix fixe, you can't go wrong here.

Shaffer City Oyster Bar & Grill Ⓢ 23 | 17 | 22 | $43
5 W. 21st St. (bet. 5th & 6th Aves.), 212-255-9827
■ "They really know their oysters" at this Flatiron "diamond-in-the-rough" boasting one of the "best bivalve selections in NYC" plus plenty of other "fantastic seafood"; "showman"-owner Jay Shaffer ("a hoot", "a darling") ensures that "the only thing bland is the dining room."

Stage Deli ◐Ⓢ 18 | 9 | 14 | $25
834 Seventh Ave. (bet. 53rd & 54th Sts.), 212-245-7850
☑ "Carnegie Deli is still the better bet", but the lines are shorter at this Midtown rival, which also sells mega sandwiches, offers litttle in the way of decor and employs "gruff" "sherpas of schmaltz" to tell the Texan tourists which is the bagel and which is the lox.

Strip House Ⓢ 24 | 23 | 21 | $56
13 E. 12th St. (bet. 5th Ave. & University Pl.), 212-328-0000
■ It's hard not to be "captivated by the sensual vibe" at this Central Villager where "sexy" red banquettes and walls with old photos of "playfully" posed strippers foreshadow

"excellent" steaks served by an "attentive staff"; in sum, a "welcome change" for the genre.

Sugiyama | 28 | 21 | 26 | $92 |
251 W. 55th St. (bet. B'way & 8th Ave.), 212-956-0670
■ Watch master sushi chef Nao Sugiyama prepare an array of "extraordinary" dishes at this "small", understated West 50s Japanese "jewel", which offers one of the "best kaiseki meals" in Manhattan; "wonderful servers" who "explain each dish thoroughly" and "say goodbye in unison" help ease the "astronomical" tab.

Supper ●⑤≠ | – | – | – | M |
156 E. Second St. (bet. Aves. A & B), 212-477-7600
The latest and largest of Frank Prisinzano's "ever-expanding East Village empire", this new Northern Italian's lively front area centered around an open kitchen and quieter back room are always packed with local hipsters tucking into bargain-priced pastas; come early or prepare to wait it out – possibly at the next-door bar/lounge, Sugo.

Sushiden | 23 | 17 | 20 | $47 |
123 W. 49th St. (bet. 6th & 7th Aves.), 212-398-2800
■ "There are never any leftovers" at this "low-key", slightly "pricey" Midtown Japanese where they "remember you after one visit"; the "broad selection" of "high-quality" "sushi made with precision" attracts "lots of businessmen" and the pre-theater crowd.

SushiSamba ●⑤ | 22 | 22 | 16 | $45 |
245 Park Ave. S. (bet. 19th & 20th Sts.), 212-475-9377
87 Seventh Ave. S. (Barrow St.), 212-691-7885
■ "Crowds as sexy as the inventive" South American–influenced Japanese food "pack" these "colorful", "loud" eateries where the cocktails are "A++", the sushi and seviches are "delectable" and the (Village branch's) rooftop garden is "like being in the tropics"; slightly "arrogant" service and "hefty tabs" come with the territory.

Sushi Zen | 25 | – | 21 | $47 |
108 W. 44th St. (bet. B'way & 6th Ave.), 212-302-0707
■ "Fresh as it gets" declare afishionados of this Japanese Theater Districter's "first-class" sushi, whose "excellence" makes the "hefty" prices "easier to swallow"; it recently moved around the corner, gaining some elbow room but losing its "great back garden."

Taka ●⑤ | 26 | 13 | 19 | $45 |
61 Grove St. (bet. Bleecker St. & 7th Ave. S.), 212-242-3699
■ Reserve at the bar or "arrive early" to avoid the "long waits" at chef-owner Takako Yoneyama's "shoebox-size" West Village Japanese where she "artfully prepares" and serves "unusual", "mouthwatering" sushi and sashimi "on her own pottery"; portions are "small" and the "decor's plainer than Nebraska", but otherwise "this place rocks."

Tamarind ●🅂   24 | 23 | 21 | $47
41-43 E. 22nd St. (bet. B'way & Park Ave. S.), 212-674-7400
■ "A relief from the stereotypical sitar-laden places", this "modern" Flatiron "haute Indian" is an "exquisite" spot for "Brahmins and their bankers" to "snag a booth" and enjoy haute-priced "refined" cooking; P.S. the next-door Tea Room "is a stellar sidekick."

Tang Pavilion 🅂   22 | 17 | 21 | $34
65 W. 55th St. (bet. 5th & 6th Aves.), 212-956-6888
■ "Solid", "high-quality" Shanghai-style cooking at modest prices, "courteous" service and a "quiet" West 50s setting just made for a "business lunch" are the "enduring" traits of this outfit; since "you can easily miss it", the "frighteningly fast" delivery comes in handy.

Tasting Room ●   26 | 17 | 25 | $51
72 E. First St. (bet. 1st & 2nd Aves.), 212-358-7831
■ "Tiny on space" but "big on taste", this must-reserve East Village New American is "like a private party"; "doting", "gracious" host Renee Alevras tends the room while husband Colin turns out "delicious", "innovative" seasonal cuisine backed by a "fantastic all-U.S. wine list."

Thalia Restaurant ●🅂   20 | 21 | 19 | $48
828 Eighth Ave. (50th St.), 212-399-4444
■ "Above-average" prix fixe lunch and dinner have made this "sleek" "high-ceilinged" New American a compelling "pre-theater" option to "share some backstage gossip" amid "attractive" lighting; the adjacent take-out branch is an office-worker "staple."

Tocqueville 🅂   24 | 21 | 23 | $61
15 E. 15th St. (bet. 5th Ave. & Union Sq. W.),
212-647-1515
■ Deserving to be better known, this "very adult" Union Square French-American is a "charming" "place to catch up with a friend" over "excellent" cooking and "well-chosen wines"; a "gracious" staff and "tremendous" prix fixe lunch fuel this "winning experience."

Tomoe Sushi   27 | 8 | 15 | $36
172 Thompson St. (bet. Bleecker & Houston Sts.),
212-777-9346
☑ "Excruciating" "hour-long waits" ("pay an NYU student to stand in line for you") and a "boring", "armpit-to-armpit" setting are easily forgiven after a taste of the "amazingly priced", "perfect cuts" of "orgasmic" sushi at this Village Japanese; it has a cult-like following, with good reason.

Topaz Thai 🅂   22 | 11 | 16 | $27
127 W. 56th St. (bet. 6th & 7th Aves.), 212-957-8020
☑ "Lots of people stand in line" for a "good", "affordable" Thai lunch or dinner "pre–Carnegie Hall" or City Center at this "tiny" Midtown outlet; "rushed", "assembly-line"

service and a "cramped" environment suggest you won't
want to linger.

Town ⑤   24 | 25 | 22 | $67
Chambers Hotel, 15 W. 56th St. (bet. 5th & 6th Aves.),
212-582-4445
■ "A hit" from day one, this Midtowner is where "beautiful
people", "power expense-accounters" and "serious diners"
sip "trendy" cocktails at the "cool bar" then descend to an
"ultra-modern" dining room to partake in Geoffrey Zakarian's
"superb" New American cooking; no surprise – it's always
"packed" and "expensive."

Trattoria Dell'Arte ⑥⑤   21 | 20 | 19 | $49
900 Seventh Ave. (bet. 56th & 57th Sts.), 212-245-9800
■ A "wonderful" antipasti bar, "excellent pizza", whimsical
"body-part" decor and a "convenient" Midtown location,
"perfect" pre– or post–City Center, are the draws at this
"bustling" Italian; its "diverse clientele" ranges from
theatergoers and tourists to business diners.

Trattoria Dopo Teatro ⑥⑤   16 | 16 | 16 | $40
125 W. 44th St. (bet. B'way & 6th Ave.), 212-869-2849
■ "Try and sit by a window to watch the world go by" or
in the "delightful" basement-level indoor garden at this
"middle-of-the-road" Theater District Italian; the "decent"
food may not wow you, but the staff will definitely "get
you out on time."

Triomphe ⑤   23 | 22 | 21 | $57
Iroquois Hotel, 49 W. 44th St. (bet. 5th & 6th Aves.),
212-453-4233
■ "Diverse", "inventive" ideas and "terrific flavors" abound
at this "elegant" New French Theater District "jewel box";
since the staff is "formal yet friendly", consider coming "for
both business and pleasure", e.g. a "leisurely" "romantic"
meal; an annex is set to open.

'21' Club   21 | 22 | 23 | $63
21 W. 52nd St. (bet. 5th & 6th Aves.), 212-582-7200
■ "Still the ultimate" "NY experience", this renowned
townhouse "institution" is seemingly "unchanged since
Prohibition" and "never goes out of style" thanks to its
"clubby" atmosphere redolent with "exclusivity", tuxedoed
"pro" service, "classic all-American" cuisine and a
"legendary" wine cellar; even though the good things come
at a price, there are prix fixe menus at lunch ($32) and
pre-theater ($37) to offer ordinary mortals the chance to
live like a "bigwig"; naturally, it's jacket-and-tie required.

Union Square Cafe ⑤   27 | 23 | 26 | $60
21 E. 16th St. (bet. 5th Ave. & Union Sq. W.), 212-243-4020
■ Still "a winner after all these years", Danny Meyer's
original "first-class restaurant" remains the place for
"all-around wonderful dining experiences" that define

"perfection without pretension", from chef Michael Romano's "deceptively simple, exquisitely satisfying" New American cuisine to the "always gracious" pro staff that "sets the NYC benchmark for great service" to the "classy but not stuffy setting."

Utsav S 21 | 20 | 18 | $35
1185 Sixth Ave. (enter on 46th or 47th St., bet. 6th & 7th Aves.), 212-575-2525
■ It may be "difficult to find", but this "posh" Midtown Indian is "worth the quest" given its "abundance" of "distinct, savory" dishes "served with charm and grace"; budget-conscious surveyors love to use this place to impress: it "looks much more expensive than it is."

Veritas S 27 | 22 | 26 | $80
43 E. 20th St. (bet. B'way & Park Ave. S.), 212-353-3700
■ "A wine list longer than the Old Testament" is the claim to fame of this Flatiron "world-class" New American, but diners who pony up for its prix fixe dinners ($68) attest to chef Scott Bryan's "perfectly executed" cuisine that "dazzles from the eye to the stomach" and proves to be "commensurate" with the "fabulous" vintages; in short, "everything about" this eatery is imbued with "intelligence."

ViceVersa 23 | 22 | 22 | $49
325 W. 51st St. (bet. 8th & 9th Aves.), 212-399-9291
■ For a "first-rate" "alternative to the same old" pasta slingers, this Hell's Kitchen "hot" spot provides "interesting", "delicious" Italian fare with "no flip side" given the "friendly pro service" and "stylish" room; a "pleasant garden" rounds out an "affordable" "surprise" that really "fills up" in the pre-show hours.

Victor's Cafe ● S 21 | 19 | 19 | $45
236 W. 52nd St. (bet. B'way & 8th Ave.), 212-586-7714
■ You don't have to go through Mexico to "sneak into Cuba", since this Theater District spot "brings you back to Havana" with "magnífico" food, "super sangria" and a "classy" pre-Fidel tropical setting; it's "a little expensive", but compadres "can't resist" the urge to splurge.

View, The S 17 | 25 | 19 | $52
Marriott Marquis Hotel, 1535 Broadway (bet. 45th & 46th Sts.), 212-704-8900
■ "Take a spin" at this "rotating" Continental atop the Times Square Marriott offering "breathtaking" views and "better-than-expected" food for those able to overlook the "touristy" milieu; theatergoers who turn out nightly attest the tabs may leave you "light-headed."

Virgil's Real BBQ S 21 | 13 | 16 | $30
152 W. 44th St. (bet. B'way & 6th Ave.), 212-921-9494
☑ "Leave your diet behind" when you mosey over to this "cholesterolicious" Times Square barbecue joint whose

"Bubba-approved" grub is "as real as it gets in the Big Apple"; it's "fun and cheap", but "dingy" digs, "noisy", "touristy" crowds and long "waits" are also part of the "finger-lickin'" experience here.

Wallsé ⑤   25 | 19 | 21 | $58

344 W. 11th St. (Washington St.), 212-352-2300

■ "Waltz over" to the West Village for Kurt Gutenbrunner's "wunderbar" "contemporary" takes on "classic Viennese" cuisine, matched by a "great Austrian wine" list and backed by an interior exuding Austrian "chic" and a "youngish", "accommodating" staff; yes, it's "expensive, but worth it" – "especially in winter."

Wu Liang Ye ⑤   21 | 12 | 15 | $26

36 W. 48th St. (bet. 5th & 6th Aves.), 212-398-2308

☑ Forget Benadryl, you're sure to "clear your sinuses" at this "authentic Szechuan" whose "addictively" "hot", "spicy" fare and low tabs ensnare plenty of "repeat customers"; if a few fuss about dreary decor and "smile"-challenged servers, most recognize the kitchen as coming in a "cut above" their peers.

Yama   25 | 11 | 15 | $36

122 E. 17th St. (Irving Pl.), 212-475-0969
38-40 Carmine St. (bet. Bedford & Bleecker Sts.), 212-989-9330 ⑤
92 W. Houston St. (bet. La Guardia Pl. & Thompson St.), 212-674-0935 ◗ ⑤

☑ "Godzilla-size", "creative", "fresh" sushi at "affordable" prices is the lure at this Japanese trio; however, "epic waits", "perfunctory service" and dull decor are obvious turnoffs, except at the "roomier Carmine Street location", which "takes reservations."

Restaurant Indexes

CUISINES
LOCATIONS
SPECIAL FEATURES

Indexes list the best of many within each category.

CUISINES

American
Amy's Bread
Angus McIndoe
Anju
Annisa
AZ
Beacon
Blue Hill
Bryant Park
Charlotte
City Bakery
Corner Bistro
Craft
District
Fives
44
44 & X
Giorgio's
Gotham B&G
Gramercy Tavern
Hourglass
Ilo
Island Burgers
Jezebel (Southern)
Joe Allen
JUdson Grill
Kitchen 22
Maxie's
Mesa Grill (Southwestern)
Noche
Norma's
One if by Land
Redeye Grill
Tasting Room
Thalia
Tocqueville
Town
'21' Club
Union Sq. Cafe
Veritas
Virgil's (Barbecue)

Asian
Anju
China Grill
Topaz Thai

Brazilian
Chur. Plataforma
Rice 'n' Beans

Californian
Martini's
Michael's

Chinese
Grand Sichuan
Tang Pavilion
Wu Liang Ye

Continental
Sardi's
View, The

Delis
Carnegie Deli
Stage Deli

Eclectic
B. Smith's
China Grill

French
Fleur de Sel
La Belle Epoque
La Caravelle
La Côte Basque
La Metairie
Le Bernardin
Le Rivage
René Pujol
Tocqueville
Triomphe

French (Bistro)
Cafe Un Deux Trois
Chez Michallet
db Bistro Moderne
Le Beaujolais
Le Madeleine
Pergola/Artistes
Pierre au Tunnel
Pigalle

Greek
Kyma
Milos
Molyvos
Periyali

Indian
Bay Leaf
Shaan

Tamarind
Utsav

Italian

(N=Northern, S=Southern)
Arezzo
Babbo
Barbetta (N)
Becco (N)
Beppe (N)
Campagna (N)
Cascina
Crispo
Cucina di Pesce
Da Tommaso (N)
Esca (S)
Fontana di Trevi (N)
Gonzo
Il Mulino (N)
Il Tinello (N)
'ino
Lanza
La Pizza Fresca (N)
La Rivista
Lattanzi (N)
Lupa
Martini's
Nocello (N)
Orso (N)
Osteria del Circo (N)
Patsy's (S)
Piccolo Angolo (N)
Pó
Remi (N)
Supper (N)
Trattoria Dell'Arte
Trattoria Dopo
ViceVersa

Japanese

Bond Street
Haru
Hasaki
Iso
Jewel Bako
Sugiyama
Sushiden
SushiSamba
Sushi Zen
Taka
Tomoe Sushi
Yama

Mediterranean

Marseille
Olives

Mexican

Hell's Kitchen
Mexicana Mama

Other

Aquavit (Scandinavian)
A Salt & Battery (English)
La Belle Epoque (Creole)
Meskerem (Ethiopian)
Victor's Cafe (Cuban)
Wallsé (Austrian)

Pizza

Angelo's Pizzeria
Cascina
Gonzo
Joe's Pizza
John's Pizzeria
La Pizza Fresca

Russian

FireBird
Russian Samovar

Seafood

Blue Fin
Blue Water Grill
Pearl Oyster
Sea Grill
Shaffer City

South American/Spanish

Bolo
Chicama
Patria
Pipa
SushiSamba

Steakhouses

Angelo & Maxie's
Ben Benson's
Cité
Cité Grill
Del Frisco's
Gallagher's
Palm West
Ruth's Chris
Strip House

LOCATIONS

East Village
(14th to Houston Sts.,
east of B'way)
A Salt & Battery
Bond Street
Cucina di Pesce
Hasaki
Iso
Jewel Bako
Lanza
Supper
Tasting Room

Flatiron District/
Union Square
(Bounded by 24th & 14th Sts.,
bet. 6th Ave. & Park Ave. S.)
Angelo & Maxie's
Anju
Arezzo
AZ
Beppe
Blue Water Grill
Bolo
Campagna
Chicama
City Bakery
Craft
Fleur de Sel
Giorgio's
Gramercy Tavern
Kitchen 22
La Pizza Fresca
Mesa Grill
Olives
Patria
Periyali
Pipa
Shaffer City
SushiSamba
Tamarind
Tocqueville
Union Sq. Cafe
Veritas
Yama

Greenwich Village
(14th to Houston Sts., bet.
B'way & 7th Ave. S., excluding
NoHo)
Annisa
Babbo

Blue Hill
Cascina
Gonzo
Gotham B&G
Il Mulino
'ino
Joe's Pizza
John's Pizzeria
La Belle Epoque
Lupa
Meskerem
One if by Land
Pearl Oyster
Pó
Strip House
SushiSamba
Tomoe Sushi
Yama

West 40s
Amy's Bread
Angus McIndoe
Barbetta
Becco
Blue Fin
Bryant Park
B. Smith's
Cafe Un Deux Trois
Cascina
Charlotte
Chur. Plataforma
db Bistro Moderne
Del Frisco's
District
Esca
FireBird
44
44 & X
Haru
Hell's Kitchen
Hourglass
Ilo
Jezebel
Joe Allen
John's Pizzeria
Kyma
La Rivista
Lattanzi
Le Beaujolais
Le Madeleine
Le Rivage
Marseille

Maxie's
Meskerem
Noche
Orso
Pergola/Artistes
Pierre au Tunnel
Pigalle
Sardi's
Sea Grill
Shaan
Sushiden
Sushi Zen
Trattoria Dopo
Triomphe
Utsav
View, The
Virgil's
Wu Liang Ye

West 50s

Angelo & Maxie's
Angelo's Pizzeria
Aquavit
Bay Leaf
Beacon
Ben Benson's
Carnegie Deli
China Grill
Cité
Cité Grill
Da Tommaso
Fives
Fontana di Trevi
Gallagher's
Grand Sichuan
Il Tinello
Island Burgers
JUdson Grill
La Caravelle
La Côte Basque
Le Bernardin

Martini's
Michael's
Milos
Molyvos
Nocello
Norma's
Osteria del Circo
Palm West
Patsy's
Redeye Grill
Remi
René Pujol
Rice 'n' Beans
Russian Samovar
Ruth's Chris
Stage Deli
Sugiyama
Tang Pavilion
Thalia
Topaz Thai
Town
Trattoria Dell'Arte
'21' Club
ViceVersa
Victor's Cafe

West Village

(14th to Houston Sts., west of
7th Ave. S., excluding
Meatpacking District)
A Salt & Battery
Chez Michallet
Corner Bistro
Crispo
La Metairie
Mexicana Mama
Piccolo Angolo
Taka
Wallsé

SPECIAL FEATURES

Child-Friendly
Amy's Bread
Cafe Un Deux Trois
Campagna
Carnegie Deli
Chur. Plataforma
Cité Grill
City Bakery
John's Pizzeria
Norma's
Patsy's
Redeye Grill
Shaffer City
Stage Deli
Virgil's

"In" Places
Annisa
AZ
Babbo
Beacon
Beppe
Blue Hill
Blue Water Grill
Bond Street
Craft
db Bistro Moderne
Esca
FireBird
Gramercy Tavern
Kitchen 22
Milos
Molyvos
Olives
Redeye Grill
Strip House
Supper
SushiSamba
Tamarind
Tasting Room
Town
Veritas
Wallsé

Late Dining
Blue Water Grill (12:30 AM)
Carnegie Deli (4 AM)
Corner Bistro (3:30 AM)
Gonzo (1 AM)
Haru (1 AM)
Joe's Pizza (5 AM)
Redeye Grill (12:30 AM)

Supper (2:45 AM)
SushiSamba (1 AM)

Outdoor Dining
(G=garden; P=patio;
S=sidewalk; T=terrace)
AZ (G)
Barbetta (G)
Bay Leaf (G)
Ben Benson's (T)
Blue Hill (G)
Blue Water Grill (T)
Bryant Park (G,P)
China Grill (S)
Cucina di Pesce (G)
Esca (P)
44 & X (S)
Hasaki (G)
La Belle Epoque (S)
Lanza (G)
Lattanzi (G)
Le Rivage (P)
Lupa (P)
Marseille (S)
Martini's (S,T)
Meskerem (S)
Milos (T)
Olives (S)
Periyali (G)
Pipa (S)
Pó (S)
Remi (G)
Sea Grill (G)
Sushi Zen (S)
Tamarind (S)
Tocqueville (S)
Trattoria Dell'Arte (S)
Utsav (P,S)
ViceVersa (G)

Quiet Conversation
Barbetta
Blue Hill
Chez Michallet
FireBird
Fleur de Sel
Gramercy Tavern
Il Tinello
La Caravelle
Le Bernardin
Norma's
One if by Land

subscribe to zagat.com

Restaurant Special Feature Index

Tocqueville
Union Sq. Cafe
Veritas

Romantic
AZ
Barbetta
Blue Hill
Chez Michallet
FireBird
Jezebel
La Côte Basque
One if by Land
ViceVersa

Sunday
(B=brunch; L=lunch;
D=dinner)
Angus McIndoe (L,D)
Annisa (D)
Aquavit (B, D)
AZ (D)
Babbo (D)
Bay Leaf (L,D)
Becco (L,D)
Ben Benson's (D)
Blue Fin (B,D)
Blue Hill (D)
Blue Water Grill (B,D)
Bolo (D)
Bond Street (D)
Bryant Park (B,D)
B. Smith's (B,D)
Cafe Un Deux Trois (B,L,D)
Campagna (D)
Carnegie Deli (B,L,D)
Charlotte (B,D)
Chez Michallet (B,D)
Chicama (D)
China Grill (D)
Chur. Plataforma (L,D)
Cité (D)
Corner Bistro (L,D)
Craft (D)
db Bistro Moderne (D)
Del Frisco's (D)
District (D)
Esca (D)
FireBird (D)
Fives (B)
Fleur de Sel (D)
Fontana di Trevi (D)
44 (B,L,D)
Giorgio's (D)

Gonzo (L,D)
Gotham B&G (D)
Gramercy Tavern (L,D)
Hasaki (D)
Hell's Kitchen (D)
Jezebel (D)
Joe Allen (B,L,D)
Kyma (L,D)
La Metairie (L,D)
La Pizza Fresca (D)
Le Beaujolais (D)
Le Madeleine (B,L,D)
Le Rivage (L,D)
Lupa (L,D)
Marseille (D)
Martini's (D)
Maxie's (L,D)
Mesa Grill (B,L,D)
Milos (D)
Molyvos (L,D)
Nocello (D)
Olives (B,D)
One if by Land (D)
Orso (B,L,D)
Osteria del Circo (D)
Palm West (D)
Patria (D)
Piccolo Angolo (D)
Pigalle (B,L,D)
Pipa (B,D)
Pó (D)
Redeye Grill (B,D)
Remi (D)
Russian Samovar (D)
Ruth's Chris (D)
Sardi's (B,L,D)
Shaan (L,D)
Strip House (D)
SushiSamba (L,D)
Tamarind (L,D)
Tang Pavilion (L,D)
Thalia (B,D)
Tocqueville (D)
Town (B,D)
Trattoria Dell'Arte (B,D)
Union Sq. Cafe (L,D)
Utsav (B,L,D)
Veritas (D)
Victor's Cafe (L,D)
View, The (B,D)
Virgil's (L,D)
Wallsé (D)

Visitors on Expense Account
Beacon
Blue Hill
Carnegie Deli
Craft
Del Frisco's
FireBird
Gotham B&G
Gramercy Tavern
Il Mulino
Ilo
La Caravelle
La Côte Basque
Le Bernardin
Mesa Grill
Milos
One if by Land
Patria
Periyali
Remi
Strip House
Sugiyama
Trattoria Dell'Arte
Union Sq. Cafe
Veritas

Nightlife

Key to Ratings/Symbols

Name, Address, Subway Stop, Phone Number & Web Site

Zagat Ratings

Credit Cards

A	D	S	C
▽ 23	5	9	$5

TIM & NINA'S ⊘

4 Columbus Circle (8th Ave.), 1/9/A/B/C/D to 59th St./ Columbus Circle, 212-977-6000; www.zagat.com

◪ Open 24/7, this "deep dive" bar with a bathroom and phone booth across the street resembles a "none-too-clean garage"; however, "dirt cheap" prices, a free-flowing tap and unlimited pretzels gratis draw "spaced-out crowds" of "multi-pierced patrons"; N.B. don't trip on any of the customers on the way out.

Review, with surveyors' comments in quotes

Before reviews a symbol indicates whether responses were uniform ■ or mixed ◪.

Credit Cards: ⊘ no credit cards accepted

Ratings: Appeal, Decor and Service are rated on a scale of **0** to **30**. The Cost (C) column reflects surveyors' estimated price of a typical single drink.

A	Appeal	D	Decor	S	Service	C	Cost
23		5		9		$5	

0–9 poor to fair
10–15 fair to good
16–19 good to very good

20–25 very good to excellent
26–30 extraordinary to perfection
▽ low response/less reliable

For places listed without ratings or a cost estimate, such as an important **newcomer** or a popular **write-in,** the cost is indicated by the following symbols.

I below $5
M $5 to $8

E $9 to $11
VE more than $11

Top Rated Nightspots

Excluding places with low votes.

Top Theater District

Overall Appeal
- *27* Rainbow Grill
- *25* Pen-Top Bar
  View Lounge

Decor
- *27* FireBird
- *26* Rainbow Grill
- *25* Library/Paramount

Service
- *22* FireBird
  Library/Paramount
- *21* Chez Josephine

Most Popular
1. Divine Bar
2. Flûte
3. Blue Fin

Top Union Square

Overall Appeal
- *25* Park Bar
- *22* Flûte
  Living Rm/W

Decor
- *23* Park Bar
- *22* Living Rm/W
  Flûte

Service
- *21* Park Bar
- *19* Flûte
  Old Town Bar

Most Popular
1. Coffee Shop
2. Flûte
3. Underbar

Top Village

Overall Appeal
- *26* Angel's Share
- *25* Bar Veloce
  Decibel

Decor
- *25* Temple Bar
- *24* Hudson Bar
- *23* Angel's Share

Service
- *23* Angel's Share
  Bar Veloce
- *21* Temple Bar

Most Popular
1. Chumley's
2. Angel's Share
3. Decibel

Top by Special Feature

Bars
- *26* Angel's Share
- *25* Park Bar
- *24* Chez Josephine
  Chumley's
- *23* Otheroom

First Date
- *26* Angel's Share
- *25* Pen-Top Bar
  Park Bar
- *24* Temple Bar
- *23* Otheroom

Grown-Ups
- *27* Rainbow Grill
- *25* Pen-Top Bar
- *24* Chez Josephine
- *23* FireBird
- *22* Blue Bar

Hotel Bars
- *25* Pen-Top Bar
  View Lounge
- *24* Cellar Bar
  Library/Paramount
- *22* Blue Bar

Lounges

26	Angel's Share
24	Temple Bar
22	Divine Bar
	Flûte
	Living Rm/W Union Sq.

Outdoors

25	Pen-Top Bar
22	Divine Bar
	Bryant Park Grill
21	Ava Lounge▽
18	Coffee Shop

Quiet Conversation

27	Rainbow Grill
26	Angel's Share
25	Decibel
24	Library/Paramount
	Temple Bar

Swanky

27	Rainbow Grill
24	Cellar Bar
23	FireBird
22	Flûte
20	Underbar

Trendy

24	Cellar Bar
22	Divine Bar
	Flûte
	Living Rm/W Union Sq.
	Blue Fin

Angel's Share
26 | 23 | 23 | $10

8 Stuyvesant St., 2nd fl. (9th St. & 3rd Ave.), 6 to Astor Pl., 212-777-5415

■ A "quiet little shrine to the humble cocktail", this "soft and sexy" East Village bar is equally known for its "hard-to-find", "hush-hush" entrance and "heavenly drinks" (courtesy of "exacting" bartenders whose "surgeon-like precision" even extends to "cutting the ice by hand"); mind the "house rules" – "no standing", "no rowdy behavior", "no groups over four" – as the payoff is a scene so "serene" that it can ignite (or "rekindle") a romance.

Arthur's Tavern ⏗
20 | 12 | 18 | $7

57 Grove St. (7th Ave. S.), 1/9 to Christopher St., 212-675-6879; www.arthurstavernnyc.com

■ Rife with "historical appeal", this "been-there-forever" Village boîte might not be "pretty", but it does supply an "always-a-party-going-on" mood; expect "awesome live" jazz and blues, "no cover" and an "unpretentious" crowd.

Ava Lounge
▽ 21 | 25 | 21 | $11

Majestic Hotel, 210 W. 55th St., 15th fl. (B'way), N/Q/R/W to 57th St., 212-956-7020; www.avaloungenyc.com

■ "As glamorous as [its namesake] Ava Gardner", this "swank" new Midtown lounge supplies some "sexy voyeurism" via its "fantastic views of Times Square – and the apartment across the street"; the pièce de résistance is an "impeccable penthouse deck" ("complete with a bed if you need a nap") that should prove to be a "hot" scene.

Babalu
20 | 20 | 19 | $10

327 W. 44th St. (bet. 8th & 9th Aves.), A/C/E to 42nd St./Port Authority, 212-262-1111; www.babaluny.com

■ The "drinks go down like fruit punch" – then "knock you on your ass" – at this "lively" Theater District Latin nightclub where the spirit of "Ricky Ricardo lives on"; fans prepared to "swivel their hips" show up for the "serious" weekend dance scene as well as the "amazing live performances."

Bar Veloce
25 | 22 | 23 | $10

175 Second Ave. (bet. 11th & 12th Sts.), L to 3rd Ave., 212-260-3200

■ "Slinky patrons" make for a "super chic" scene at this "fabulous" albeit "teeny" East Village wine bar that's "perfect date bait"; the "mod mood" is revved up by a "no-miss" vino list, "sublime panini", "enthusiastic bartenders" and "Italian movies on the overhead widescreen."

Blue Bar
22 | 21 | 21 | $11

Algonquin Hotel, 59 W. 44th St. (bet. 5th & 6th Aves.), 7/B/D/F/V to 42nd St./6th Ave., 212-840-6800; www.algonquinhotel.com

■ "Suckers for history" "escape into reverie" at this venerable Midtown hotel bar, a "cozy, literate" hangout that's "old school in the best possible way"; granted, it might be a "little musty" for teenier boppers, but there's no better place in inclement weather to "slip out of your wet clothes into a dry martini" and truly "feel like an adult."

Blue Fin   22 | 24 | 19 | $11

W Times Square Hotel, 1567 Broadway (47th St.), N/R/W to 49th St., 212-918-1400; www.brguestrestaurants.com

■ "Times Square needed" a "hip, modern spot" and now has one in this "swimming" yearling from Steve Hanson laid out on two levels: downstairs is a "happening" if "tight" bar (with "glass walls" offering streetside people-watching), while upstairs there's "more room" and an "ice-topped" counter to keep your drinks cold; either way, this "perfect complement" to the Theater District delivers some "heavy action in the center of the universe."

Broadway Lounge   ▽ 22 | 19 | 21 | $12

Marriott Marquis Hotel, 1535 Broadway, 8th fl. (bet. 45th & 46th Sts.), 1/2/3/7/9/N/Q/R/S/W to 42nd St./Times Sq., 212-398-1900; www.nymarriottmarquis.com

◪ "Mostly for tourists", this Marriott Marquis bar/lounge purveys the "most magnificent view of Times Square" (so long as you snag a table close to the windows); since it "doesn't revolve like it used to", some find "nothing special" going on besides its definite "NYC atmosphere."

Bryant Park Cafe/Grill   22 | 19 | 15 | $9

25 W. 40th St. (behind NY Public Library), 7/B/D/F/V to 42nd St./ 5th Ave., 212-840-6500; www.arkrestaurants.com

■ For a NY experience "par excellence", it's "hard to beat" this "splendid" alfresco cafe in Bryant Park (and its indoor bistro sibling) where "power suits" convene for "outside imbibing" while exchanging "business cards" and cell phone numbers with "pretty" gals; though the "mosh pit"– like "overcrowding" makes for "not enough seats or servers", "no one wants to leave" this fine example of "summer in the city."

Carnegie Club   ▽ 23 | 23 | 23 | $12

156 W. 56th St. (bet. 6th & 7th Aves.), N/Q/R/W to 57th St., 212-957-9676

■ "Like its location, the crowd is in its 50s" at this "stylish" Midtowner where the "mature" go to be "pampered" and listen to "smoky standards" by "live singers and jazzy bands"; the "warm lighting makes anyone look like a million", which is close to "what you'll spend for a scotch" and soda here.

Cellar Bar   24 | 25 | 19 | $12

Bryant Park Hotel, 40 W. 40th St., downstairs (bet. 5th & 6th Aves.), 7/B/D/F/V to 42nd St./Bryant Park, 212-642-2136; www.thebryantpark.net

■ "Away from the bright lights and big city" off Bryant Park lies this "fairly undiscovered" subterranean hideaway, one of the "sexiest" bars in town owing to a "dark, mysterious" aesthetic and a "Guastavino-esque vaulted ceiling"; more "subdued" than lively, it draws "bigwig" "international" types who love the "soft, jazzy music" and don't think twice about the "sooo expensive" tabs.

Chez Josephine   24 23 21 $11
414 W. 42nd St. (bet. 9th & 10th Aves.), A/C/E to 42nd St./ Port Authority, 212-594-1925

■ "Romantic to the nth degree", this 42nd Street shrine to Josephine Baker is operated by her "fabulous" adopted son, Jean-Claude; "very French" digs and "live piano music" make it a "perfect stop-off" "pre- or post-theater."

China Club   20 19 17 $10
268 W. 47th St. (bet. B'way & 8th Ave.), C/E to 50th St., 212-398-3800; www.chinaclubnyc.com

☑ "Celebs grace the VIP lounge" while "bystanders try to get noticed" at this Theater District duplex, a longtime "pretty people" magnet that's become a "staple" over the years, and legendary for its "hot Monday night" parties; while trendoids sigh it's "not cool anymore" ("can you say 1989?"), its "standing-room-only" status suggests the scene's as "noisy, energetic and wild" as ever.

Chumley's ⌀   24 19 18 $7
86 Bedford St. (bet. Barrow & Grove Sts.), 1/9 to Christopher St., 212-675-4449

■ There are "few better places on a cold winter's night" than this West Village "former speakeasy", a "bar that time forgot", where the fireplace crackles and it always "smells like Christmas dinner"; famously "difficult to find", it's home to a mix of tourists, "frat boys" and firemen drawn by its "character" and "charm."

Code   _ _ _ M
(fka Chase)
255 W. 55th St. (bet. B'way & 8th Ave.), N/Q/R/W to 57th St., 212-333-3400

Midtowners wet their whistles at this new duplex lounge offering a variety of semi-private areas including a petite downstairs den made for stolen kisses; with the nearby arrivals of Ava Lounge and Divine Bar West, this nondescript nightlife nabe is becoming a drinker's destination.

Coffee Shop   18 15 13 $9
29 Union Sq. W. (16th St.), 4/5/6/L/N/Q/R/W to 14th St./ Union Sq., 212-243-7969

☑ "After clubbing all night", this 23/7 Union Square Brazilian is a "happening enough" destination that "looks like a diner, but acts like a bar"; though "not as trendy as it used to be", it still attracts a "cross section of too-cool-to-care" types (and some "uncool", "sunglasses-at-night" wearers), all moaning about the "crappy service" and "clueless" staff.

Cutting Room | 20 | 17 | 18 | $8 |
19 W. 24th St. (bet. B'way & 6th Ave.), N/R to 23rd St.,
212-691-4065; www.thecuttingroomnyc.com
■ "Owned by Mr. Big himself", this "low-key" Flatiron
lounge supplies Chris Noth and other "star sightings" along
with "top-notch cocktails", "Ms. Pac-Man", "live music"
and "bizarre cabaret" in its back room; though it "can get
crowded" with spillover from Eugene next door, this "great
scene" is always "lots of fun."

Decibel | 25 | 17 | 19 | $9 |
240 E. Ninth St. (bet. 2nd & 3rd Aves.), 6 to Astor Pl., 212-979-2733
■ Imagine a "little bar on a Tokyo sidestreet" to get the gist
of this "intimate" East Village "basement" lounge exuding
a "speakeasy feel" thanks to a "door buzzer"–required
entry; inside, a "punked-out Japanese staff" serves "every
kind of sake you can imagine", though its "boho" fan base
has three words of advice: "lychee martinis, baby!"

Divine Bar | 22 | 21 | 20 | $9 |
236 W. 54th St. (bet. B'way & 8th Ave.), C/E to 50th St.,
212-265-9463
■ "Take off on a wine flight" at this "high-class" Midtowner,
the "perfect starting point for a girls' night out" given
its "heavenly" vino selection matched by "yummy hors
d'oeuvres" and "fun fondue"; while "downstairs is a busy
after-work" terrain compared to the "more romantic"
upstairs, either way "be prepared to stumble out afterward."

Eau | ▽ 22 | 22 | 19 | $11 |
913 Broadway, 2nd fl. (bet. 20th & 21st Sts.), N/R to 23rd St.,
212-358-8647
■ "Slammin' drinks" and "jammin' DJs" make for sometimes
"cramped" conditions at this aquatic-themed Flatiron
lounge; the "minimalist" setting (including a water-lined bar
and zeppelin-shaped ceiling fans) makes the "expensive"
cocktails easier to swallow.

FireBird Cafe | 23 | 27 | 22 | $12 |
365 W. 46th St. (bet. 8th & 9th Aves.), A/C/E to 42nd St./
Port Authority, 212-586-0244
■ One part "Russian museum", one part "cabaret", this
"high-class" Restaurant Row boîte offers "phenomenal"
entertainment washed down with one of the "best selections
of vodka" around; dissidents say *nyet* to the "give-me-a-
break" pricing, but comrades counter where else can you
"feel like a tsar might walk in at any moment"?

Flatiron Lounge | – | – | – | E |
37 W. 19th St. (bet. 5th & 6th Aves.), 1/9 to 18th St., 212-727-7741
An original, circa-1927 art deco bar rings nostalgic notes at
this Flatiron newcomer where the self-described 'gourmet
cocktails for foodies' are expertly concocted (mixologist

Dale DeGroff is a consultant); a tribute to the glory days of sophisticated imbibing, this lounge is sweetened by low music made for romancing.

Flûte   22 | 22 | 19 | $11

205 W. 54th St. (bet. B'way & 7th Ave.), N/Q/R/W to 57th St., 212-265-5169
40 E. 20th St. (bet. B'way & Park Ave. S.), 6 to 23rd St., 212-529-7870
www.flutebar.com

■ "Lovebirds frolic" and "smooch" at these "classy" champagne "make-out" lounges purveying a "large selection of bubbly" and a "quieter vibe than most NY spots"; Midtown's "subterranean" speakeasy layout might be "sexier" than that of its three-story Flatiron sibling, but either way, "dress up" and bring the big "checkbook."

Grey Dog's Coffee ⊄   23 | 21 | 21 | $6

33 Carmine St. (bet. Bedford & Bleecker Sts.), 1/9 to Christopher St., 212-462-0041

■ "Villagers and visitors alike" dig this slice of "California cool", a "laid-back neighborhood" coffeehouse that's "almost smaller than a breadbox" yet a "great alternative to Starbucks"; it serves "cheap" beer and wine as well as caffeine – and "you can bring your dog with you."

Hudson Bar & Books   22 | 24 | 20 | $11

636 Hudson St. (bet. Horatio & Jane Sts.), A/C/E/L to 14th St./ 8th Ave., 212-229-2642

■ "Pretend you're in your own private library" and "curl up with a good drink" at this West Village boîte that might be "more bar than books" but certainly has the "dark, romantic" thing down pat; it's a "low-key" locus for a chat or a date, though some wish they'd "turn down the music and turn up the snack portions."

Il Posto Accanto   – | – | – | E

190 E. Second St. (bet. Aves. A & B), F/V to Lower East Side/ 2nd Ave., 212-228-3562

"One of the best neighborhood wine bars", this East Villager offers intimate, "first date"–worthy surroundings, "knowledgeable, friendly bartenders" and an "owner who treats you as a guest in his home" – now, if only they'd fix that "uncomfortable seating."

Library at the Paramount   24 | 25 | 22 | $11

Paramount Hotel, 235 W. 46th St. (bet. B'way & Eighth Ave.), A/C/E to 42nd St./Port Authority, 212-764-5500; www.ianschragerhotels.com

■ Hotelier Ian Schrager hits the mark with this "lovely" "upscale" bar on the Paramount's mezzanine where "pretty people" sip "pricey" potables; since the "B&T crowd has moved on" to trendier pastures, its "uncrowded" yet "visually compelling" ambiance just might help you "score."

Living Room at the W Times Square
— — — E

W Times Square Hotel, 1567 Broadway (47th St.), N/R to 49th St., 212-930-7444; www.midnightoilbars.com
Sleek as sleek can be, this Times Square lounge is a magnet for the suits-and-stilettos crowd who like its streamlined, very W Hotel design; fly barmaids serving killer cocktails keep it kicking, but killer costs cause critics to choke.

Living Room at the W Union Square
22 22 18 $11

W Union Square Hotel, 201 Park Ave. S. (17th St.), 4/5/6/L/ N/Q/R/W to 14th St./Union Sq., 212-353-8345
▇ The W Union Square adds its "cachet" to the "hotel lobby concept" at this "swank" bar/lounge where the "'in' crowd" vies to "score" a couch for a session of "watching the pretty people"; though nonfans note it's "overpriced" and the staff "overrun", it's more down to earth than Underbar, its hyper-hip subterranean sibling.

M Bar
— — — E

Mansfield Hotel, 12 W. 44th St. (bet. 5th & 6th Aves.), 7/B/ D/F/V to 42nd St./6th Ave., 212-277-8888; www.mansfieldhotel.com
"Tucked away" yet near the "heart of Times Square", this "cozy" hotel bar "looks like a library" and "feels like an oasis" thanks to a "relaxingly friendly" atmosphere that's both grown-up and "urban"; "very, very quiet", it works for a "rendezvous" or a "private conversation" and draws an "interesting mix" of Euros, business types and incognito, poorly disguised philanderers.

Noche
23 24 20 $10

1604 Broadway (bet. 48th & 49th Sts.), 1/9 to 50th St.; N/R/ W to 49th St., 212-541-7070
■ "Festivities" with a "Latin flair" get under way at this "spectacular" new Times Square arrival that "lives up to its hype" with a streetside bar and a "hot, happening" "multilevel" upstairs where a "big stage" anticipates the "Ricky Ricardo of the new millennium"; "delicious" drinks add *vida* to the *noche,* and with a cabaret license on the way, samba mania "can't wait" to "kick off."

Old Town Bar
21 16 19 $6

45 E. 18th St. (bet. B'way & 5th Ave.), 4/5/6/L/N/Q/R/W to 14th St./Union Sq.; N/R to 23rd St., 212-529-6732
■ Flatiron's "real deal" in "old-school" saloons, this wood-boothed "perennial" is a "time machine" from 1892 where "diehards" park themselves at the "ancient oak bar" to "drink, not be seen" as they "stare down" curious "young" pups and yups; so "untouched" it seems ready to "crumble", it's a "landmark" of "dissipated" charm with "not an ounce of pretense" and "no cell phones" permitted ("perfect!").

Otheroom ⌐   23 | 19 | 20 | $7
143 Perry St. (bet. Greenwich & Washington Sts.), 1/9 to Christopher St., 212-645-9758

■ Take a date and "cozy up" at this "teeny" West Village beer-and-wine dispenser that maintains the "right decibel level" and such a "sexy" ambiance that those who "snag a seat" on the "secluded" "couch in back" may "never get up"; it's a "neighborhood find" that's "not easy to find", and keepers of the "secret" plead "don't tell!"

Park Bar   25 | 23 | 21 | $8
15 E. 15th St. (bet. 5th Ave. & Union Sq. W.), 4/5/6/L/N/Q/R/ W to 14th St./Union Sq., 212-367-9085

■ "The secret's out" on this "classy little" "diamond in the rough" near Union Square, a "sophisticated", "antiquish nook" where "dark" wood, a tiled floor and a "wonderful staff" lend a "certain charm" for "30s" scenesters; it's a "perfect" spot for parking with a date – if you can "find a seat, that is."

Pen-Top Bar   25 | 20 | 20 | $13
Peninsula Hotel, 700 Fifth Ave., 23rd fl. (55th St.), E/V to 5th Ave./ 53rd St., 212-903-3097; www.peninsula.com

■ Take in "spectacular skyline" views at this literally "high-end" "conversation bar" atop a Midtown hotel, rising 23 floors closer to "heaven" with a "bustling, open-air" terrace and "holy-cow" prices that might "make you want to jump"; the "corporate crowd" is glad to "pay a premium" to "feel this fabulous", so "get there early" 'cause tables "go fast" in warm weather.

Rainbow Grill   27 | 26 | 20 | $15
30 Rockefeller Plaza, 65th fl. (49th St.), B/D/F/V to 47-50th Sts./ Rockefeller Ctr., 212-632-5145; www.cipriani.com

■ "Get a second job" to finance a visit to this "venerable" Rockefeller Center "refuge from the madding crowds", providing "unbeatable" top-of-the-world views from a swank "art deco" roost with piano accompaniment to enhance the "romance"; sightseeing "tourists" and "outta-sight" prices are irksome, but with that "quintessential skyline" vista, "who cares?"

Royalton Round Bar   ▽ 26 | 26 | 19 | $13
Royalton Hotel, 44 W. 44th St. (bet. 5th & 6th Aves.), 7/B/D/ F/V to 42nd St./Bryant Park, 212-869-4400; www.ianschragerhotels.com

■ "Squeeze" into this "darling" "little jewel box" of a bar tucked behind a curved wall in the Royalton Hotel lobby with a "genie bottle design", leather-padded walls and a vodka-and-champagne drink menu; it's a "no-brainer" for an "intimate", "sexy" rendezvous, but such a "popular hideaway" with so few seats that you could be pitching woo standing up.

Russian Samovar
19 | 15 | 17 | $9
256 W. 52nd St. (bet. B'way & 8th Ave.), C/E to 50th St., 212-757-0168
■ "Stoli meets Baskin-Robbins" at this Theater District Russian bar/restaurant with an "unbelievable array of flavored vodkas" ("dispensed from little spigots") that puts patrons in a "blissful stupor"; *da,* there's "no visual appeal", but at least the pianist "gets better with every shot."

Russian Vodka Room
22 | 16 | 19 | $9
265 W. 52nd St. (bet. B'way & 8th Ave.), C/E to 50th St., 212-307-5835
■ "Say *dosvedanya* to sobriety" at this "sleazy, boozy" Theater District "Moscow on the Hudson" famed for its "heavenly but deadly" vodka infusions and "dodgy" "peroxide blonde" clientele; maintaining the "perfect level of dinginess", this "wild and wooly Russki" "time warp" is just the place to propose "something illicit."

SBNY ⌦
22 | 20 | 20 | $8
(aka Splash)
50 W. 17th St. (bet. 5th & 6th Aves.), F/N/R/V to 23rd St., 212-691-0073; www.splashbar.com
■ "It's raining men" at this Flatiron gay bar "winner" where "go-go boys in bikini bottoms" grind "for your pleasure" and "drop-dead gorgeous bartenders" stir loins as well as drinks; despite equally "stiff" covers, this "muscles-and-martinis" mainstay "still packs them in" for "heavy-duty cruising", though chances are good you'll "pick up a tourist from Indiana."

Shelly's New York
21 | 20 | 21 | $11
104 W. 57th St. (6th Ave.), F to 57th St., 212-245-2422; www.shellysnewyork.com
■ Though it's "too cool" for the "dull neighborhood of Midtown", this "not widely known", second-floor boîte is a sweet spot to "grab an after-work cocktail" with the added premium of "live jazz"; throw in some "really good raw seafood snacks" and it's no surprise that many "can't just go there for drinks" and wind up downstairs for a "fabulous" meal.

Show
- | - | - | E
(fka Saci)
135 W. 41st St. (bet. B'way & 6th Ave.), 1/2/3/7/9/N/Q/R/S/W to 42nd St./Times Sq., 212-278-0988; www.shownightclub.com
One part ballroom-style performance venue, one part disco-ball dance club, this new Theater District extravaganza is spread out over multi-levels, all focused around a stage headlining entertainment that's a mix of the Moulin Rouge, Weimar-era cabaret and Times Square vaudeville; no surprise, scenesters are show-ing up in droves.

Single Room Occupancy ▽ 24 24 25 $10
(aka SRO)
360 W. 53rd St. (bet. 8th & 9th Aves.), C/E to 50th St., 212-765-6299

■ There's "hope for Midtown" via this "wonderful secret" in Hell's Kitchen that's a "challenge to find" what with the "speakeasy-like entrance" and buzzer for admittance; once inside, you'll find a "tiny, narrow" "converted basement" bar that serves only "beer and wine", but its "cozy" ambiance and rotating artwork more than compensate.

Temple Bar 24 25 21 $10
332 Lafayette St. (bet. Bleecker & Houston Sts.), 6 to Bleecker St., 212-925-4242

■ "Finish the night" with a "little nuzzling" at this "sultry", "low-lit" NoHo sanctuary where the extra "sexy vibe" sets the scene for a "stylish tryst" or clinking "well-mixed" martinis with a "hot stranger"; the "decadent speakeasy" feel means twosomes can get to be "more than just friends", so "dress nice" and prepare to flash "lots of cash" – it's really "worth it."

Xth Ave Lounge 21 23 17 $8
642 10th Ave. (bet. 45th & 46th Sts.), A/C/E to 42nd St./ Port Authority, 212-245-9088

■ "Come as you are" to this "far west Hell's Kitchen" haunt for "all lifestyles", where a "mixed straight and gay crowd" chills out to the nth degree in "classy, laid-back" quarters complete with "dark corners" and "cool blue-lit bathrooms"; it's a "non-sceney" rendezvous where "young-at-heart" "cuties" can "meet up" and x-plore the possibilities.

Twist Lounge – – – E
Ameritania Hotel, 230 W. 54th St. (bet. B'way & 8th Ave.), 1/9/A/B/C/D to 59th St./Columbus Circle, 212-247-5000; www.nychotels.com

The retro set's "best-kept secret" may be this "side bar in the lobby" of a Midtown hotel, where a "tiny, mod" room done up in white vinyl provides an "ultrasmooth" backdrop for a "chat" over martinis; swingers say the "luxurious" flash is "kinda fun", though on the "overpriced" side.

Underbar 20 21 15 $10
W Union Square Hotel, 201 Park Ave. S. (bet. 17th & 18th Sts.), 4/5/6/L/N/Q/R/W to 14th St./Union Sq., 212-358-1560; www.midnightoilbars.com

◪ Those who "feel like posing" with "Euro-ish" patrons and "model wanna-be" staffers head for this subterranean "playground" at the W Union Square Hotel, a "dark, swanky" lair with a "center-of-the-room bed", "curtained-off" "private cubbies" and "throbbing music"; those who are underwhelmed shrug "overdone" and "overplayed", and "air kiss" it goodnight.

View Lounge
25 | 23 | 16 | $11

Marriott Marquis Hotel, 1535 Broadway, 48th fl. (bet. 45th & 46th Sts.), 1/2/3/7/9/N/Q/R/S/W to 42nd St./Times Sq., 212-704-8900; www.nymarriottmarquis.com
■ "Round and round" goes the "revolving lounge" atop this Theater District hotel, where the "spectacular view" draws attention from the "somewhat lacking" amenities and "overpriced" drinks; regarded locally as a "dizzy novelty", it's a "must-visit for tourists" with an all-you-can-eat buffet and dance floor worthy of "Club Med."

Whiskey, The
21 | 21 | 18 | $11

W Times Square Hotel, 1567 Broadway, downstairs (47th St.), N/R to 49th St., 212-930-7444; www.midnighttoilbars.com
■ So "very 'in'" "it aches", this "hopping" Times Square club is "swarming with pretty young things" and the "almost famous", all looking "gorgeous" glued to "their cells"; the "pristine" space showcases "cool gimmicks" like a "lit-up" dance floor with "squishy" *Saturday Night Fever* tiles and "signature coed bathrooms", but "bring big bucks" and beware "pseudo-exclusive attitude" and "wanna-be chic."

Zanzibar
21 | 20 | 18 | $9

645 Ninth Ave. (45th St.), A/C/E to 42nd St./Port Authority, 212-957-9197; www.zanzibarnyc.com
◪ "Youngish MTV types" zanz options can be found "chatting away" over "fabulous" drinks at this "chic" but "mellow" Hell's Kitchen lounge, a "competent effort" with "velvet chairs" and a "circular fireplace"; if scenemakers sigh it's "too far to trek" for a taste of "Downtown attitude", it still beats "the Irish pubs in the area."

Nightlife
Indexes

CATEGORIES
LOCATIONS
SPECIAL APPEALS

CATEGORIES

Bar
Angel's Share
Arthur's Tavern
Babalu
Blue Bar
Blue Fin
Carnegie Club
Cellar Bar
Chez Josephine
Chumley's
Coffee Shop
Flatiron Lounge
Hudson Bar
Library/Paramount
Living Rm/W Times Sq.
Living Rm/W Union Sq.
M Bar
Noche
Old Town Bar
Otheroom
Park Bar
Pen-Top Bar
Royalton Bar
Russian Samovar
Russian Vodka Rm
SBNY

Coffeehouse
Grey Dog's

Hotel Bars
Algonquin Hotel
  Blue Bar
Ameritania Hotel
  Twist Lounge
Bryant Park Hotel
  Cellar Bar
Majestic Hotel
  Ava Lounge
Mansfield Hotel
  M Bar

Marriott Marquis Hotel
  B'way Lounge
  View Lounge
Paramount Hotel
  Library/Paramount
Peninsula Hotel
  Pen-Top Bar
Royalton Hotel
  Royalton Bar
W Times Square Hotel
  Blue Fin
  Living Rm/W Times Sq.
  Whiskey, The
W Union Square Hotel
  Living Rm/W Union Sq.
  Underbar

Lounge
Angel's Share
B'way Lounge
Carnegie Club
Cellar Bar
Cutting Room
Divine Bar
Eau
Flatiron Lounge
Flûte
Hudson Bar
Library/Paramount
Living Rm/W Times Sq.
Living Rm/W Union Sq.
Otheroom
Shelly's NY
Temple Bar
Xth Ave Lounge
Twist Lounge
Underbar
View Lounge
Whiskey, The
Zanzibar

LOCATIONS

MANHATTAN

East Village
(14th to Houston Sts., east of B'way)
Angel's Share
Bar Veloce
Decibel
Il Posto

Flatiron District/Union Square
(Bounded by 24th & 14th Sts., bet. 6th Ave. & Park Ave. S.)
Coffee Shop
Cutting Room
Eau
Flatiron Lounge
Flûte
Living Rm/W Union Sq.
Old Town Bar
Park Bar
SBNY
Underbar

Greenwich Village
(14th to Houston Sts., bet. B'way & 7th Ave. S., excluding NoHo)
Arthur's Tavern
Grey Dog's

NoHo
(Bet. 4th & Houston Sts., bet. Bowery and W. B'way)
Temple Bar

West 40s
Babalu
Blue Bar
Blue Fin

B'way Lounge
Bryant Park Grill
Cellar Bar
Chez Josephine
China Club
FireBird
Library/Paramount
Living Rm/W Times Sq.
M Bar
Noche
Rainbow Grill
Royalton Bar
Show
Xth Ave Lounge
View Lounge
Whiskey, The
Zanzibar

West 50s
Ava Lounge
Carnegie Club
Code
Divine Bar
Flûte
Pen-Top Bar
Russian Samovar
Russian Vodka Rm
Shelly's NY
Single Room Occu.
Twist Lounge

West Village
(14th to Houston Sts., west of 7th Ave. S., excluding Meatpacking District)
Chumley's
Hudson Bar
Otheroom

SPECIAL APPEALS

For multi-location nightspots, the availability of index features may vary by location.

For some categories, schedules may vary; call ahead or check Web sites for the most up-to-date information.

Drink Specialists
Beer
Otheroom
Champagne
Cellar Bar
Flûte
Royalton Bar
Cocktails
Angel's Share
Flatiron Lounge
M Bar
Russian Vodka Rm
Temple Bar
Whiskey, The
Zanzibar
Sake
Decibel
Wine Bars
Bar Veloce
Divine Bar
Il Posto
Wine by the Glass
Otheroom
Shelly's NY
Single Room Occu.

First Date
Angel's Share
Il Posto
Otheroom
Park Bar
Pen-Top Bar
Royalton Bar
Temple Bar
Zanzibar

Grown-Ups
Blue Bar
Carnegie Club
Chez Josephine
FireBird
M Bar
Pen-Top Bar
Rainbow Grill

Noteworthy Newcomers
Ava Lounge
Code
Noche
Show

Outdoor Spaces
(* Rooftop)
Ava Lounge*
Bryant Park Grill
Divine Bar
Pen-Top Bar*

Quiet Conversation
Angel's Share
Decibel
FireBird
Flûte
Hudson Bar
Il Posto
Library/Paramount
M Bar
Otheroom
Rainbow Grill
Temple Bar
Twist Lounge

Swanky
Ava Lounge
Carnegie Club
Cellar Bar
FireBird
Flûte
Rainbow Grill
Royalton Bar

Trendy
Ava Lounge
Blue Fin
Cellar Bar
Divine Bar
Flûte
Living Rm/W Union Sq.
Show
Underbar

Hotels

Algonquin
59 W. 44th St.; 212-840-6800; fax 212-944-1419; 800-555-8000;
www.algonquinhotel.com; 174 rooms (24 suites)

Benjamin
125 E. 50th St.; 212-715-2500; fax 212-715-2525; 888-423-6526;
www.thebenjamin.com; 209 rooms (98 suites)

Bryant Park
40 W. 40th St.; 212-869-0100; fax 212-869-4446;
877-640-9300; www.thebryantpark.net; 129 rooms
(20 suites)

Carlyle
35 E. 76th St.; 212-744-1600; fax 212-717-4682;
800-227-5737; www.thecarlyle.com; 180 rooms (56 suites)

Chambers
15 W. 56th St.; 212-974-5656; fax 212-974-5657;
866-204-5656; www.chambersnyc.com; 77 rooms (5 suites)

City Club
55 W. 44th St.; 212-921-5500; fax 212-575-2758;
www.cityclubhotel.com; 65 rooms

DoubleTree Guest Suites
1568 Broadway; 212-719-1600; fax 212-921-5212;
800-222-8733; www.doubletree.com; 460 suites

Elysée
60 E. 54th St.; 212-753-1066; fax 212-980-9278;
800-535-9733; www.elyseehotel.com; 101 rooms (15 suites)

Embassy Suites
102 North End Ave.; 212-945-0100; fax 212-945-3012;
800-362-2779; www.embassysuites.com; 463 suites

Essex House
160 Central Park S.; 212-247-0300; fax 212-315-1839;
800-937-8461; www.essexhouse.com; 605 rooms (80 suites)

Four Seasons
57 E. 57th St.; 212-758-5700; fax 212-758-5711;
800-332-3442; www.fourseasons.com; 368 rooms
(63 suites)

Hilton New York
1335 Sixth Ave.; 212-586-7000; fax 212-315-1374;
www.hilton.com; 1,990 rooms (47 suites)

Hilton Times Square
234 W. 42nd St.; 212-930-7400; fax 212-930-7500;
877-946-8357; www.hilton.com; 509 rooms (43 suites)

Hudson
356 W. 58th St.; 212-554-6000; fax 212-554-6139;
800-444-4786; www.ianschragerhotels.com; 1,000 rooms

Inn at Irving Place
56 Irving Pl.; 212-533-4600; fax 212-533-4611; 800-685-1447; www.innatirving.com; 12 rooms (6 suites)

Inter-Continental
Central Park South
112 Central Park S.; 212-757-1900; fax 212-757-9620; 800-327-0200; www.interconti.com; 211 rooms (21 suites)

Inter-Continental Barclay
111 E. 48th St.; 212-755-5900; fax 212-644-0079; 800-327-0200; www.interconti.com; 687 rooms (84 suites)

Iroquois
49 W. 44th St.; 212-840-3080; fax 212-719-0006; 800-332-7220; www.iroquoisny.com; 114 rooms (9 suites)

Kitano
66 Park Ave.; 212-885-7000; fax 212-885-7100; 800-548-2666; www.kitano.com; 131 rooms (18 suites)

Le Parker Méridien
118 W. 57th St.; 212-245-5000; fax 212-708-7471; 800-543-4300; www.parkermeridien.com; 730 rooms (100 suites)

Library
299 Madison Ave.; 212-983-4500; fax 212-499-9099; 877-793-7323; www.libraryhotel.com; 60 rooms (8 suites)

Lowell
28 E. 63rd St.; 212-838-1400; fax 212-319-4230; 800-221-4444; www.lhw.com; 68 rooms (47 suites)

Mark
25 E. 77th St.; 212-744-4300; fax 212-744-2749; 800-843-6275; www.mandarinoriental.com; 177 rooms (60 suites)

Marriott Brooklyn
333 Adams St., Brooklyn; 718-246-7000; fax 718-246-0563; 800-228-9290; www.marriott.com; 376 rooms (21 suites)

Marriott Marquis
1535 Broadway; 212-398-1900; fax 212-704-8930; 800-228-9290; www.marriott.com; 1,949 rooms (61 suites)

Mercer
147 Mercer St.; 212-966-6060; fax 212-965-3838; 888-918-6060; www.mercerhotel.com; 75 rooms (7 suites)

Michelangelo
152 W. 51st St.; 212-765-1900; fax 212-581-7618; 800-237-0990; www.michelangelohotel.com; 178 rooms (55 suites)

Millennium Broadway
145 W. 44th St.; 212-768-4400; fax 212-768-0847; 800-622-5569; www.millenniumhotels.com; 752 rooms (14 suites)

Millennium UN Plaza
1 United Nations Plaza; 212-758-1234; fax 212-702-5048;
866-866-8086; www.millennium-hotels.com; 427 rooms
(45 suites)

Morgans
237 Madison Ave.; 212-686-0300; fax 212-779-8352;
800-334-3408; www.ianschragerhotels.com; 113 rooms
(22 suites)

Muse
130 W. 46th St.; 212-485-2400; fax 212-485-2900;
877-485-2400; www.themusehotel.com; 200 rooms
(16 suites)

New York Palace
455 Madison Ave.; 212-888-7000; fax 212-303-6000;
800-697-2522; www.newyorkpalace.com; 896 rooms
(84 suites)

Omni Berkshire Place
21 E. 52nd St.; 212-753-5800; fax 212-754-5020;
800-843-6664; www.omnihotels.com; 396 rooms (47 suites)

Paramount
235 W. 46th St.; 212-764-5500; fax 212-354-5237;
800-225-7474; www.ianschragerhotels.com; 601 rooms
(12 suites)

Peninsula
700 Fifth Ave.; 212-956-2888; fax 212-903-3949;
800-262-9467; www.peninsula.com; 239 rooms (55 suites)

Phillips Club
155 W. 66th St.; 212-835-8800; fax 212-835-8850;
877-854-8800; www.phillipsclub.com; 180 suites

Pierre
2 E. 61st St.; 212-838-8000; fax 212-940-8109; 800-743-7734;
www.fourseasons.com; 201 rooms (51 suites)

Plaza Athénée
37 E. 64th St.; 212-734-9100; fax 212-772-0958;
800-447-8800; www.plaza-athenee.com; 152 rooms
(35 suites)

Plaza
768 Fifth Ave.; 212-759-3000; fax 212-759-3167;
800-759-3000; www.fairmont.com; 805 rooms (96 suites)

Regency
540 Park Ave.; 212-759-4100; fax 212-826-5674;
800-233-2356; www.loewshotels.com; 351 rooms (87 suites)

Regent Wall Street
55 Wall St.; 212-845-8600; fax 212-845-8601; 800-545-4000;
www.regenthotels; 144 rooms (47 suites)

Renaissance
714 Seventh Ave.; 212-765-7676; fax 212-765-1962;
800-468-3571; www.renaissancehotels.com; 305 rooms
(5 suites)

RIHGA Royal
151 W. 54th St.; 212-307-5000; fax 212-765-6530;
800-937-5454; www.marriott.com; 500 suites

Ritz-Carlton Battery Park
2 West St.; 212-344-0800; fax 212-344-3804; 800-241-3333;
www.ritzcarlton.com; 298 rooms (44 suites)

Ritz-Carlton, Central Park
50 Central Park S.; 212-308-9100; fax 212-207-8831;
800-241-3333; www.ritzcarlton.com; 277 rooms (40 suites)

Royalton
44 W. 44th St.; 212-869-4400; fax 212-869-8965;
800-635-9013; www.ianschragerhotels.com; 169 rooms
(27 suites)

Sheraton Manhattan
790 Seventh Ave.; 212-581-3300; fax 212-541-9219;
888-625-5144; www.starwood.com; 666 rooms (4 suites)

Sherry-Netherland
781 Fifth Ave.; 212-355-2800; fax 212-319-4306; 800-247-4377;
www.sherrynetherland.com; 62 rooms (33 suites)

60 Thompson
60 Thompson St.; 212-431-0400; fax 212-431-0200;
877-431-0400; www.60thompson.com; 100 rooms (10 suites)

SoHo Grand
310 W. Broadway; 212-965-3000; fax 212-965-3200;
800-965-3000; www.sohogrand.com; 379 rooms (4 suites)

Stanhope Park Hyatt
995 Fifth Ave.; 212-774-1234; fax 212-517-0088;
800-223-1234; www.hyatt.com; 185 rooms (57 suites)

St. Regis
2 E. 55th St.; 212-753-4500; fax 212-787-3447; 800-759-7550;
www.stregis.com; 314 rooms (92 suites)

Surrey
20 E. 76th St.; 212-288-3700; fax 212-628-1549;
800-637-8483; www.mesuite.com; 131 suites

Swissôtel – The Drake
440 Park Ave.; 212-421-0900; fax 212-371-4190;
888-737-9477; www.swissotel.com; 495 rooms (108 suites)

TriBeCa Grand
2 Sixth Ave.; 212-519-6600; fax 212-519-6700; 877-519-6600;
www.tribecagrand.com; 203 rooms (7 suites)

Trump International
1 Central Park W.; 212-299-1000; fax 212-299-1150;
888-448-7867; www.trumpintl.com; 167 rooms (167 suites)

Waldorf-Astoria & Towers
301 Park Ave.; 212-355-3000; fax 212-872-7272;
800-925-3673; www.hilton.com; 1,425 rooms (250 suites)

Warwick
65 W. 54th St.; 212-247-2700; fax 212-247-2725;
800-223-4099; 422 rooms (60 suites)

Westin New York at Times Square
270 W. 43rd St.; 212-201-2700; fax 212-201-2701;
800-937-8461; www.westinny.com; 863 rooms (31 suites)

W New York
541 Lexington Ave.; 212-755-1200; fax 212-319-8344;
877-946-8357; www.whotels.com; 714 rooms (61 suites)

W The Court
120 E. 39th St.; 212-686-1600; fax 212-779-0148;
877-946-8357; www.whotels.com; 198 rooms (40 suites)

W Times Square
1567 Broadway; 212-930-7400; fax 212-930-7500;
888-625-5144; www.whotels.com; 466 rooms (43 suites)

W Union Square
201 Park Ave. S.; 212-253-9119; fax 212-253-9229;
877-946-8357; www.whotels.com; 270 rooms (17 suites)

Parking Facilities

THEATER DISTRICT

Advance Parking
249 W. 43rd St. (bet. 7th & 8th Aves.), 212-221-8902

Astor Parking
1511 Broadway (45th St.), 212-869-3543

Burlington House Garage
101-41 W. 54th St. (bet. 6th & 7th Aves.), 212-245-8708

Central Parking System
330 W. 44th St. (bet. 8th & 9th Aves.), 212-757-8375
332-344 W. 44th St. (bet. 8th & 9th Aves.), 212-247-5807
253 W. 47th St. (bet. B'way & 8th Ave.), 212-582-5711
132-146 W. 51st St. (bet. 6th & 7th Aves.), 212-241-7418
31 W. 52nd St. (bet. 5th & 6th Aves.), 212-246-9256
810 Seventh Ave. (bet. 52nd & 53rd Sts.), 212-581-5215
880-888 Eighth Ave. (bet. 52nd & 53rd Sts.), 212-245-0068
159 W. 53rd St. (bet. 6th & 7th Aves.), 212-245-1299
235 W. 56th St. (bet. B'way & 8th Ave.), 212-974-6147

Chap-Sun Garage
148 W. 48th St. (bet. 6th & 7th Aves.), 212-575-9133

Circle Parking
200 W. 52nd St. (bet. B'way & 7th Ave.), 212-397-9029

City Spire Garage
156 W. 56th St. (bet. 6th & 7th Aves.), 212-265-0841

Command Parking
1700 Broadway (54th St.), 212-664-9042

Direct Parking
51 W. 56th St. (bet. 5th & 6th Aves.), 212-664-8564

Eastway Tenant
225-231 W. 49th St. (bet. B'way & 8th Ave.), 212-262-9779

Edison 42nd Parking
427 W. 42nd St. (bet. 9th & 10th Aves.), 212-279-5213

Edison Parking Mgmt.
600-650 W. 42nd St. (11th Ave.), 212-643-8178

1114 Sixth Parking
1114 Sixth Ave. (bet. 42nd & 43rd Sts.), 212-768-7843

Friars 50th St. Garage
218 W. 50th St. (bet. B'way & 8th Ave.), 212-262-9795

Garment Garage
252 W. 40th St. (bet. 7th & 8th Aves.), 212-840-2270

Global Parking
143 W. 40th St. (bet. B'way & 7th Ave.), 212-221-9485

Hudson View Garage
747 10th Ave. (bet. 50th & 51st Sts.), 212-974-9608

Icon Parking
1330 Sixth Ave. (bet. 53rd & 54th Sts.), 212-586-0169
230 W. 55th St. (bet. B'way & 8th Ave.), 212-399-3260
440 W. 57th St. (bet. 9th & 10th Aves.), 212-765-7069

Irene Garage
145 W. 47th St. (bet. 6th & 7th Aves.), 212-869-5479

Kinney System
101 W. 53rd St. (bet. 6th & 7th Aves.), 212-586-7000
888 Seventh Ave. (bet. 56th & 57th Sts.), 212-586-3665

Meyers Parking System
141 W. 43rd St. (bet. B'way & 6th Ave.), 212-997-7690

MTP Operating
514 W. 49th St. (bet. 10th & 11th Aves.), 212-575-7777

Park Right
600 11th Ave. (bet. 44th & 45th Sts.), 212-459-9003

Park-Serv
140 W. 53rd St. (bet. 6th & 7th Aves.), 212-397-9028

Rapid Park 411
156 W. 55th St. (bet. 9th & 10th Aves.), 212-265-7854

Sample Garage Associates
38 W. 46th St. (bet. 5th & 6th Aves.), 212-719-5944

Solo 9 West 57
9 W. 57th St. (bet. 5th & 6th Aves.), 212-754-4077

Sylvan 53 Street Garage
354 W. 53rd St. (bet. 8th & 9th Aves.), 212-397-7255

Theater Parking
415 W. 45th St. (9th & 10th Aves.), 212-265-0774

304 Associates
304 W. 49th St. (8th Ave.), 212-246-8535

330 W. 56th St. Garage
330 W. 56th St. (bet. 8th & 9th Aves.), 212-245-6883

Times Square Garage
220 W. 41st St. (bet. 7th & 8th Aves.), 212-730-1777

Top of the Line Garage
201 W. 48th St. (B'way), 212-586-0665

Triple Eight Garage
1633 Broadway (bet. 50th & 51st Sts.), 212-445-0011

West 56 Garage
211 W. 56th St. (bet. B'way & 7th Aves.), 212-262-2600

WL 56 Parking
101 W. 56th St. (bet. 6th & 7th Aves.), 212-246-4645

Zenith Parking
301 W. 51st St. (8th Ave.), 212-581-8490

UNION SQUARE

110 E. 16th St. Associates
110 E. 16th St. (bet. Irving & Union Sq. E.), 212-473-9522

202 E. 18th Street Parking
201 E. 17th St. (bet. 2nd & 3rd Aves.), 212-995-0937

Union Square Car Park
1 Irving Pl. (15th St.), 212-677-2026

THE VILLAGE

Central Parking System
91-133 Bleecker St. (Mercer St.), 212-253-9061
18-20 Morton St. (bet. Bleecker St. & 7th Ave. S.), 212-242-8451

Charles Street Garage
99 Charles St. (bet. Bleecker & Hudson Sts.), 212-242-9723

Meat Mkt. Garage
26 Little W. 12th St. (bet. Greenwich & Washington Sts.),
212-242-9860

Mercer Parking Garage
165-167 Mercer St. (bet. Prince & W. Houston Sts.), 212-226-5578

Minetta Lane Garage
122 W. 3rd St. (bet. MacDougal St. & 6th Ave.), 212-777-3530

Mutual Parking Perry St.
166-172 Perry St. (bet. Joe DiMaggio Hwy. & Washington St.),
212-741-9773

Perry Garage
738 Greenwich St. (bet. Perry & W. 11th Sts.), 212-242-8762

61 Jane Parking
61 Jane St. (Hudson St.), 212-243-6303

Thompson Street Parking
221 Thompson St. (bet. Bleecker & W. 3rd Sts.), 212-677-8741

396 Hudson Street Parking
388 Hudson St. (W. Houston St.), 212-414-4447

Travelers Garage
160 W. 10th St. (bet. Waverly Pl. & 7th Ave. S.), 212-929-3041